NATIONAL GEOGRAPHIC DIRECTIONS

OAXACA JOURNAL

OAXACA JOURNAL

——⟫⟫⟫⟫⟫⟫•⟪⟪⟪⟪⟪——

OLIVER SACKS

NATIONAL GEOGRAPHIC DIRECTIONS

NATIONAL GEOGRAPHIC
Washington, D.C.

Text copyright © 2002 Oliver Sacks
Map copyright © 2002 National Geographic Society
Illustrations copyright © 2002 Dick Rauh

First printing March 2002
Paperback edition 2005, ISBN 0-7922-4208-4

Fern drawings by Dick Rauh
Photograph on page 68 from *Strasburger's Textbook of Botany*
Excerpt on pages 126-7 by Anthony F. Aveni originally appeared in *Natural History,* April 2001.

Library of Congress Cataloging-in-Publication Data
    Sacks, Oliver W.
    Oaxaca journal / Oliver Sacks.
    p. cm.—(National Geographic directions)
    ISBN 0-7922-6521-1
    1. Oaxaca de Juarez (Mexico)—Description and travel. 2. Ferns—Mexico. 3. Sacks, Oliver W.—Journeys—Mexico. I. Title II. Series.

    F1391.O12 S23 2002
    587'.0972'74—dc21   2001057920

Founded in 1888, the National Geographic Society is one of the largest nonprofit scientific and educational organizations in the world. It reaches more than 285 million people worldwide each month through its official journal, NATIONAL GEOGRAPHIC, and its four other magazines; the National Geographic Channel; television documentaries; radio programs; films; books; videos and DVDs; maps; and interactive media. National Geographic has funded more than 8,000 scientific research projects and supports an education program combating geographic illiteracy.

For more information, please call 1-800-NGS LINE (647-5463) or write to the following address:
National Geographic Society
1145 17th Street N.W.
Washington, D.C. 20036-4688 U.S.A.

Log on to nationalgeographic.com; AOL Keyword: NatGeo.

Printed in the U.S.A

For the American Fern Society
and for plant hunters, birders, divers, stargazers,
rock hounds, fossickers, amateur naturalists
the world over.

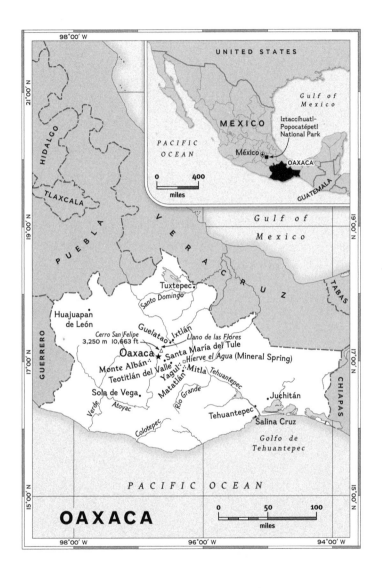

98°00′ W

21°00′ N

UNITED STATES

*Gulf of
Mexico*

MEXICO

Iztaccíhuatl-
Popocatépetl
National Park

*PACIFIC
OCEAN*

México

OAXACA

0   400
miles

GUATEMALA

19°00′ N

*Gulf of
Mexico*

HIDALGO

TLAXCALA

P U E B L A

V
E
R
A
C
R
U
Z

TABAS

17°00′ N

GUERRERO

Tuxtepec

Santo Domingo

Huajuapan
de León

Guelatao Ixtlán

Llano de las Flores

Cerro San Felipe
3,250 m 10,663 ft

Oaxaca

Santa María del Tule

Monte Albán

Hierve el Agua (Mineral Spring)

Teotitlán del Valle

Yagul Mitla

Tehuantepec

Sola de Vega

Matatlán

Río Grande

Juchitán

Verde *Atoyac*

Tehuantepec

Salina Cruz

Colotepec

*Golfo de
Tehuantepec*

CHIAPAS

15°00′ N

PACIFIC OCEAN

OAXACA

0   50   100
miles

98°00′ W   96°00′ W   94°00′ W

contents

PREFACE

I used to delight in the natural history journals of the nine-teenth century, all of them blends of the personal and the scientific—especially Wallace's *The Malay Archipelago,* Bates's *Naturalist on the River Amazon,* and Spruce's *Notes of a Botanist,* and the work which inspired them all (and Darwin too), Humboldt's *Personal Narrative.* It pleased me to think that Bates, Spruce, and Wallace were all crisscrossing in one anoth-er's paths, leapfrogging, on the same stretch of the Amazon during the selfsame months of 1849, and to think that all of them were good friends. (They continued to correspond throughout their lives, and Wallace was to publish Spruce's *Notes* after his death.)

They were all, in a sense, amateurs—self-educated, self-motivated, not part of an institution—and they lived, it sometimes seemed to me, in a halcyon world, a sort of Eden, not yet turbulent and troubled by the almost murderous rivalries which were soon to mark an increasingly professionalized world (the sort of rivalries so vividly portrayed in H. G. Wells's story "The Moth").

This sweet, unspoiled, preprofessional atmosphere, ruled by a sense of adventure and wonder rather than by egotism and a lust for priority and fame, still survives here and there, it seems to me, in certain natural history societies, and amateur societies of astronomers and archaeologists, whose quiet yet essential existences are virtually unknown to the public. It was the sense of such an atmosphere that drew me to the American Fern Society in the first place, and that incited me to go with them on their fern-tour to Oaxaca early in 2000.

And it was the wish to explore this atmosphere which, in part, incited me to keep a journal there. There was much else, of course: my introduction to a people, a country, a culture, a history, of which I knew almost nothing—this was wonderful, an adventure in itself—and the fact that all journeys incite me to keep journals. Indeed, I have been keeping them since the age of fourteen, and in the year and a half since my visit to Oaxaca, I have been in Greenland and Cuba, fossil hunting in Australia, and looking at a strange neurological condition in Guadeloupe—all of these travels have generated journals, too.

None of these journals has any pretension to comprehensiveness or authority; they are light, fragmentary, impressionistic, and, above all, personal.

Why do I keep journals? I do not know. Perhaps primarily to clarify my thoughts, to organize my impressions into a sort of narrative or story, and to do this in "real time," and not in retrospect, or imaginatively transformed, as in an autobiography or novel. I write these journals with no thought of publication (journals which I kept in Canada and Alabama were only published, and that by chance, as articles in *Antaeus,* thirty years after they were written).

Should I have prettied up this journal, elaborated it, made it more systematic and coherent—as I was to do with my book-sized Micronesian and "leg" journals—or left it as written, as with my Canadian and Alabaman ones? I have, in fact, taken an intermediate course, adding a little (on chocolate, rubber, things Mesoamerican), making little excursions of various sorts, but essentially keeping the journal as written. I have not even attempted to give it a proper title. It was Oaxaca Journal in my notebook, and *Oaxaca Journal* it remains.

O. W. S.
December 2001

CHAPTER ONE

FRIDAY

I am on my way to Oaxaca to meet up with some botanical friends for a fern foray, looking forward to a week away from New York's icy winter. The plane itself—an AeroMexico flight—has an atmosphere quite unlike anything I've ever seen. We are scarcely off the ground before everyone gets up—chatting in the aisles, opening bags of food, breast-feeding babies—an instant social scene, like a Mexican café or market. One is already in Mexico as soon as one boards. The seat-belt signs are still on, but nobody pays any attention to them. I have had a little of this feeling on Spanish and Italian planes, but it is far more marked here: this instant fiesta, this sunny laughing atmosphere all round me. How crucial it is to see other cultures, to see how special, how local they are, how un-universal one's own is. What a rigid, joyless atmosphere there is, in contrast, on most North American flights. I begin to think I will enjoy this visit. So little enjoyment, in a sense, is "permitted" these days—and yet, surely, life should be enjoyed?

My neighbor, a jolly businessman from Chiapas, wishes me *"Bon appetit!"* then the Spanish version of this, *"¡Buen provecho!"* when the meal comes. I cannot read anything on the menu, so I say yes to what I am first offered—a mistake, for it turns out to be an empanada whereas I wanted the chicken or fish. My shyness, my inability to speak other languages, alas, is a problem. I dislike the empanada, but eat some as part of my acculturation.

My neighbor asks why I am visiting Mexico, and I tell him I am part of a botanical tour headed for Oaxaca, in the south. There are several of us on this plane from New York, and we will meet up with the others in Mexico City. Learning that this is my first visit to Mexico, he speaks glowingly of the country, and lends me his guidebook. I must be sure to visit the enormous tree in Oaxaca—it is thousands of years old, a famous natural wonder. Indeed, I say, I have known of this tree and seen old photos of it since I was a boy, and this is one of the things that has drawn me to Oaxaca.

The same kind neighbor, noticing that I have torn out the end pages, and even the title page, of a book proof in order to write on them, and that I am now looking worried and out of paper, offers me two sheets from a yellow pad (I stupidly placed my own yellow pad and a notebook in my main luggage).

Observing that I said yes when asked about the empanada, obviously having no idea what it was, and then as obviously disliking it when it came, my neighbor has again lent me his guidebook, suggesting that I look at the bilingual glossary of

Mexican foods and the illustrations that go with this. I should be careful, for example, to distinguish between *atún* and *tuna,* for the Spanish word *tuna* does not denote tuna fish, but the fruit of a prickly pear. Otherwise I will keep getting fruit when I want fish.

Finding a section in the guidebook on plants, I ask him about *Mala mujer,* bad woman, a dangerous-looking tree with nettlelike stinging hairs. He tells me that youths in small-town dancing halls throw branches of it around to get the girls, everyone, scratching. This is something between a joke and a crime.

"Welcome to Mexico!" my companion says as we touch down, adding, "You will find much that is unusual and of great interest." As the plane draws to a halt he gives me his card. "Phone me," he says, "if there is any way I can be of help while you are visiting our country." I give him my address—I have to write it on a coaster, not having a card. I promise to send him one of my books, and when I see his middle name is Todd ("my grandfather came from Edinburgh"), I tell him about Todd's palsy—a brief paralysis which sometimes follows an epileptic seizure—and promise to include a short bio of Dr. Todd, the physician who first described it.

I am very touched by the sweetness and courtesy of this man. Is this a characteristic Latin American courtesy? A personal one? Or just the sort of brief encounter which happens on trains and planes?

We have a leisurely three hours in Mexico City airport—lots of time before our connection to Oaxaca. As I go to have lunch with two of the group (scarcely known to me as yet—but we will know each other well after a few days), one of them casts an eye on the little notebook I am clutching. "Yes," I answer, "I may keep a journal."

"You'll have plenty of material," he rejoins. "We're as odd a group of weirdos as you're likely to find."

No, a splendid group, I find myself thinking—enthusiastic, innocent, uncompetitive, united in our love for ferns. Amateurs—lovers, in the best sense of the word—even though a more-than-professional knowledge, a huge erudition, is possessed by a good many of us. He asks me about my own special fern interests and knowledge. "Not me...I'm just going along for the ride."

In the airport we meet up with a huge man, wearing a plaid shirt, a straw hat and suspenders, just in from Atlanta. He introduces himself—David Emory—and his wife, Sally. He was at college with John Mickel (our mutual friend, who has organized this trip), he tells me, back in '52, at Oberlin. John was an undergrad then, David a grad student. He was the one who turned John onto ferns. He is looking forward to meeting up with John when we get to Oaxaca, he says. They have only seen each other two or three times since they were schoolmates, nearly fifty years ago. They meet, each time, on botanical expeditions, and the old friendship, the old enthusiasm, is back straightaway. Time and space are annulled as they meet, converging as they do from different time zones and places, but at one in their love, their passion, for ferns.

I confess that, even more than ferns, my own preference is for the so-called fern allies: clubmosses (*Lycopodium*), horsetails

(*Equisetum*), spike mosses (*Selaginella*), whisk ferns (*Psilotum*). There would be plenty of those, too, David assures me: A new species of lycopodium was discovered on the last Oaxaca trip in 1990, and there are many species of selaginella; one, the "resurrection fern," is to be seen in the market, a flattened, seemingly dead rosette of dull green which comes to startling life as soon as it rains. And there are three equisetums in Oaxaca, he adds, including one of the largest in the world. "But psilotum," I say eagerly, "what about psilotum?" Psilotum, too, he says—two species, no less.

Even as a child, I loved the primitive horsetails and clubmosses, for they were the ancestors from which all higher plants had come.* Outside the Natural History Museum (in London, where I grew up) there was a fossil garden, with the fossilized trunks and roots of giant clubmosses and horsetails, and inside were dioramas reconstructing what the ancient forests of the Paleozoic might have looked like, with giant horsetail trees a hundred feet high. One of my aunts had shown me modern horsetails (only two feet high) in the forests of Cheshire, with their stiff, jointed stems, their knobby little cones on top. She had shown me tiny clubmosses and selaginellas, too, but she could not show me the most primitive of all, for psilotum does not grow in England. Plants resembling it—psilophytes—were the pioneers, the first land plants to develop a vascular system for transporting water through their stems, enabling them to stake a claim to the solid earth 400 million years ago, and paving the way for everything else. Psilotum, though sometimes called whisk fern, was not really a fern at all, for it had no proper roots or fronds, just an undifferentiated forking green stem, little thicker than a pencil lead. But despite its humble appearance, it was one of my favorites, and one day, I had promised myself, I would see it in the wild.

I grew up in the 1930s in a house whose garden was filled with ferns. My mother preferred them to flowering plants, and though we had roses trellised up the walls, the greater part of the flower beds was given over to ferns. We also had a glassed-

* Or so it was said when I was a boy. The current understanding, based on DNA sequencing, and not just on morphology, or the sequence of ancient plants in the fossil record, is against any such simple lineage, but indicates instead that lycopods, ferns (including fern allies), and seed plants constitute the three main lineages of vascular plants, all presumably evolved from a common ancestor back in the Silurian.

in conservatory, always warm and humid, where a great tassel fern hung, and delicate filmy ferns and tropical ferns could be grown. Sometimes on Sundays, my mother or one of her sisters, also botanically inclined, would take me to Kew Gardens, and here for the first time I saw towering tree ferns crowned with fronds twenty or thirty feet above the ground, and simulacra of the fern gorges of Hawaii and Australia. I thought these places the most beautiful I had ever seen.

My mother and my aunts had acquired their enthusiasm for ferns from their father, my grandfather, who came to London from Russia in the 1850s, when England was still in the throes of pteridomania—the great Victorian fern craze. Innumerable houses, including the one they grew up in, had their own terraria —Wardian cases—filled with varied and sometimes rare and exotic ferns. The fern craze was largely over by 1870 (not least because it had driven several species to extinction), but my grandfather had kept his Wardian cases till his death, in 1912.

Ferns delighted me with their curlicues, their croziers, their Victorian quality (not unlike the frilled antimacassars and lacy curtains in our house). But at a deeper level, they filled me with wonder because they were of such ancient origin. All of the coal that heated our home, my mother told me, was essentially composed of ferns or other primitive plants, greatly compressed, and one could sometimes find their fossils by splitting coal balls. Ferns had survived, with little change, for a third of a billion years. Other creatures, like dinosaurs, had come and gone, but ferns, seemingly so frail and vulnerable, had survived all the vicissitudes, all the extinctions the earth had known. My sense of a prehistoric world, of immense spans of time, was first stimulated by ferns and fossil ferns.

"What gate do we go from?" everyone is asking. "It's Gate 10," someone says. "They told me it was Gate 10."

"No, it's Gate 3," someone else says, "It's up there on the board, Gate 3." Yet another person has been told we are leaving from Gate 5. I have an odd feeling that the gate number is still, at this point, indeterminate. One thought is that there are only *rumors* of gate numbers until, at a critical point, one number wins. Or that the gate is indeterminable in a Heisenbergian sense, only becoming determinate at the final moment (which, if I have the right phrase, "collapses the wave function"). Or that the plane, or its probability, leaves from several gates simultaneously, pursuing all possible paths to Oaxaca.

Slight tension, hanging around, the gate finally resolved, awaiting the boarding call. Our plane was supposed to leave at 4:45 p.m., and now it is 4:50 and we have not even been boarded. (The plane, though, is here, waiting outside.) More meetings, encounters. There are nine of us now, or rather, eight of them—and me. For I have now retracted a little from the group, and am sitting a few yards from them, scribbling in my notebook.

There is almost always this doubleness, that of the participant-observer, as if I were a sort of anthropologist of life, of terrestrial life, of the species *Homo sapiens*. (This, I suppose, is why I took Temple Grandin's words as the title of *An Anthropologist on Mars,* for I, no less than Temple, am a sort of anthropologist, an "outsider," too.) But is this not so of every writer as well?

Finally, we board. My new traveling companion, not part of our group, is an elderly bald man, heavy-lidded, with an Edward VII beard, who asks for a Diet Coke with rum (I am sipping a tomato juice, primly). I raise my eyebrows. "Keeps the calories down," he jokes.

"Why not a diet rum, too?" I rejoin.

5:25 p.m.: We taxi endlessly about the monstrous tarmac, jolt-ingly, too joltingly for me to write. This giant city, God help it, has a population of 18 million (or 23 million, according to another estimate), one of the largest, dirtiest cities in the world.

5:30 p.m.: We're off! As we rise above the smear of Mexico City, which seems to stretch from one horizon to the other, my companion suddenly says, "See that…that volcano? It is called Ixtaccihuatl. Its summit is always covered in snow. There, next to it, is Popocatépetl, its head in the clouds." Suddenly, he is a different man, proud of his land, wanting to show it, explain it, to a stranger.

It is an incredible view of Popocatépetl, its caldera nakedly visible and next to it a range of high peaks covered with snow. I am puzzled that these should be snow-covered, while the higher, volcanic cone is not—perhaps there is sufficient volcanic heat, even when it is not erupting, to melt the snow. With these amazing, magical peaks all around, one sees why the ancient Aztec capital of Tenochtitlán was established here, at 7,500 feet.

My companion (now on his second rum and coke, in which I join him) inquires why I have come to Mexico. Business? Tourism? "Neither, exactly," I say. "Botany. A fern tour." He is intrigued, speaks of his own fondness for ferns. "They say," I add, "that Oaxaca has the richest fern population in Mexico."

My companion is impressed. "But you will not confine yourself to ferns?" He speaks then, with eloquence and passion, of pre-Columbian times: the astonishing sophistication of the Maya in mathematics, astronomy, architecture; how they discovered zero long before the Arabs; the richness of their art and symbolism; and how the city of Tenochtitlán had more than 200,000 people. "More than London, Paris, more than any other city on Earth at the time, except the capital of the Chinese empire." He speaks of the health and strength of the natives, how athletes would run in relays four hundred kilometers without stopping, from Tenochtitlán to the sea, so that the royal family could have fresh fish every day. About the Aztec's amazing communication network, surpassed only by that of the Inca in Peru. Some of their knowledge, some of their achievements, he concluded, seem superhuman, as if they were indeed Children of the Sun, or visitors from another planet.

And then—does every Mexican know, dwell in, his own history like this, this aching consciousness of the past?—and then came Cortés and the conquistadors, bringing not only new weapons but new sicknesses to a people who had never known them: smallpox, tuberculosis, venereal diseases, even flu. There were fifteen million Aztec in Mexico before the Conquest, but within fifty years only three million—poor, degraded, enslaved—were left. Many had been killed outright, but even more had succumbed, defenseless, to the diseases imported by the Europeans. The native religion and culture were diluted and impoverished too, replaced by the foreign traditions and churches of the conquistadors. But along with this came a rich and fertile mixing, a miscegenation which was cultural as well as physical. My neighbor goes on to speak of the "double nature, the double culture," of Mexico, the Mexicans, the complexities, positive and negative, of such a "double history." And then, as we are landing, he speaks of Mexico's political structures and institutions, their corruptness and inefficiency, and the extreme inequity of income, how Mexico has more billionaires than any other country save the U.S., but also more people living in desperate poverty.

As we descend from the plane in Oaxaca city I can see John and Carol Mickel—my friends from the New York Botanical Garden—waiting in the airport. John is an expert on the ferns of the New World, of Mexico in particular. He has discovered more than sixty new species of fern in the province of Oaxaca alone and (with his younger colleague Joseph Beitel) described its seven hundred-odd species of fern in their book *Pteridophyte Flora of Oaxaca, Mexico.* He knows where each of these ferns is to be found—their sometimes secret, or shifting, locations— better than anyone. John has been to Oaxaca many times since his first trip in 1960, and it is he who has arranged this expedition for us.

While his special expertise lies in systematics, the business of identifying and classifying ferns, tracing their evolutionary relationships and affinities, he is, like all pteridologists, an all-round botanist and ecologist too, for one cannot study ferns in the wild without some understanding of why they grow where they do, and their relationship to other plants and animals, their habitats. Carol, his wife, is not a professional botanist, but her own enthusiasm, and her many years with John, have made her almost as knowledgeable as he is.

I first met John and Carol on a Saturday morning back in 1993. I lived in the Bronx quite near the New York Botanical Garden, and that particular Saturday, I was strolling around the gardens with my friend Andrew. We happened into the old museum building, and Andrew, who had heard me rhapsodize about ferns more than once, spotted a notice referring to a meeting that day of the American Fern Society. I was curi-ous—I had never heard of it—so we wandered through the labyrinthine innards of the building and eventually found the meeting, a gathering of about three dozen people in an upstairs room. This gathering had a strangely old-fashioned, Victorian quality about it. It could have been a meeting of an amateur botanical society in the 1850s or 1870s. John Mickel, I later learned, was one of the very few professional botanists in the group.

Andrew whispered to me, "These are your sort of people," and, as usual, he was right. They were indeed my sort of people—and they seemed to recognize me, welcome me, as one of themselves, as a fern person.

It was a curious, motley crowd. In general it was an older group, with many retired people, but there were several people in their twenties too, some of whom worked in the conservatory or the horticultural parts of the garden. Some were professionals —physicians or teachers; several were housewives; one was a bus driver. Some were city dwellers, with window boxes in their apartments; others had large gardens or even greenhouses in the country. Fern passion, it was clear, respected none of the usual categories, could take hold of anyone, at any age, and claim part of their lives. Some, I would find, had driven sixty or seventy-five miles to be there.

I often have to go to professional meetings, meetings of neurologists or neuroscientists. But the feeling of this meeting was utterly different: There was a freedom, an ease and lack of competitiveness I had never seen in a professional meeting. Perhaps because of this ease and friendliness, the botanical passion and enthusiasm that everyone shared, perhaps because I felt no professional obligation resting on me, I began going to these meetings regularly, every month. Prior to this I had not belonged, with any conviction, to any group or society; now I eagerly looked forward to the first Saturday of each month; I had to be out of the country, or very sick, to miss the monthly AFS meeting.

The New York chapter was established by John Mickel in 1973, but the American Fern Society itself goes back to the 1890s, when it was founded by four amateur botanists, who stayed in touch by full and frequent letters. These letters were published by one of them as the *Linnaean Fern Bulletin,* and this soon attracted interest among fern lovers all over the country.

Amateurs, then, started the American Fern Society, just as they had founded the Torrey Botanical Society—a more general botanical society under the aegis of the famous botanist John Torrey—a few years earlier; and as they had started the British Pteridological Society in the 1890s. Most of the AFS's membership, a century later, is still made up of amateurs, with just a sprinkling of professionals. But such amateurs! There is old Tom Morgan, whom I saw at my first meeting in 1993, and whom I have seen at virtually every meeting since. Tom, who has a long white beard, and looks more than a little like Darwin, is enormously knowledgeable and indefatigable, despite having had Parkinson's disease for some years, and, recently, a broken hip. None of this daunts him: He climbs in the Adirondacks and the Rockies, treks through the rain forests of Hawaii and Costa Rica—always with his camera and notebook, recording new species and hybrids (an *Asplenium* hybrid he discovered, *Asplenium* x *morganii*, was named after him), unusual locations of ferns, strange associations of ferns with other plants and particular habitats, and unusual cultural uses of ferns (the eating of fiddleheads in different cultures, for instance, or the drinking of *Ophioglossum* tea). He is the epitome, as Darwin himself was, of the amateur naturalist, and at the same time he is perfectly at home with the latest in evolutionary theory and genetics. And yet all this is a hobby, a sideline for Tom, who was a physicist, a pioneer in materials science. Tom has been to Oaxaca, and urges me to go on this trip, even though he himself will not—he is going to Puerto Rico this year instead.

In fieldwork, field science, amateurs still provide major contributions, as they have done for centuries. In the eighteenth century, many of these amateurs were clergymen, like the Reverend William Gregor, who discovered the new element titanium in a black sand in a nearby parish, or Gilbert White, whose *Natural History of Selbourne* is still one of my favorite books. A special power of observing and remembering particulars, a special memory for places, allied to a love, a lyrical feeling for nature, is characteristic of this naturalist's sort of mind. In the 1830s it was remarked of William Smith, the "father of geology," that, even in his old age, his "memory for localities was so exact that he has often, after many years, gone direct to some hoard of nature to recover his fossils." It is similar with Tom Morgan—he remembers, I think, every fern of significance he has ever seen, and not only remembers it, but exactly where it was located.

Comets and supernovae are frequently spotted first by amateur astronomers (one such, a minister in Australia, using only a small telescope but able to remember the exact location of every supernova, has made a unique survey of the incidence of supernovae in a thousand galaxies). Amateurs are vital in mineralogy—independent of grants or professional support, they get to places professionals may not reach and describe new species of mineral every year. It is similar with fossil hunting, and bird-watching. In all of these fields, what is most crucial is not necessarily professional training but the naturalist's eye, which comes from some combination of native disposition, biophilia, with experience and passion. Amateurs, in the best sense, have exactly this—a passion, a love, for their subject, and the accumulated experience, often, of a lifetime of acute observation in the field. The professionals in the Fern Society have always recognized this, and thus everyone—so long as they love ferns—is welcome in the group, even if they are quite inexperienced. "The veriest greenhorn and the highest authority have always been on an equal footing as members," as the Society's president wrote on its fortieth anniversary—and I, as a start, am just such a greenhorn.

CHAPTER TWO

SATURDAY

ost of the thirty people on this tour to Oaxaca are members of the AFS, but drawn from different parts of the country—New York, Los Angeles, Montana, Atlanta. Today, on our first morning in Oaxaca, we are beginning to get acquainted over breakfast, and looking forward to getting our first glimpse at the town itself, an old colonial capital surrounded by a modern city of 400,000 people or so.

As we wind down the steep road from the hotel above the city, on our little tour bus, we stop and get out to enjoy a panoramic view of the city. Luis—our tour guide for the next week—points out the innumerable churches and the confines of the old colonial city. No one pays the least attention. John Mickel instantly scans the roadside for ferns, but John D. Mitchell, his near namesake and fellow botanist at the New York Botanical Garden, has an eye out for birds as well. The near identity of the two names, John Mickel and John Mitchell, is causing amusement and confusion among us, as indeed it does at the NYBG, where they both work, and where phone calls and mail for one are constantly misdirected to the other. Many of us begin to refer to John Mitchell as J.D., to distinguish him from John Mickel. Not that there is any similarity except in name. John Mickel is sixty-something, clean-shaven, lean and wiry, with tufted gray eyebrows and blue eyes; he goes bareheaded in all weather. J.D. is a younger and much larger man, and sports a huge beard. His massive head in a broad-brimmed hat, and binoculars invariably around his neck, he somewhat resembles Professor Challenger in *The Lost World*. Botanist he may be, but my first experience of J.D., today, is of a passionate, lyrical bird-watcher. He spots a bird and points it out excitedly.

"That's a dusky, a dusky hummingbird, going out of the *Ipomoea*," he whispers. "Isn't that neat?...Uh-oh! That's a yellow-rumped warbler roughing around there, going after insects."

Scott Mori (who, I learn later, is also from the NYBG, and president this year of the Torrey Botanical Society) scrambles down a precipice to get a wild tobacco plant. He examines it and murmurs, "*Nicotiana glauca.*" Though there is a *Nicotiana africana,* Scott says, the use of *Nicotiana* as tobacco came wholly from the New World, and goes back at least two thousand years.

As we pile back on the bus to continue into town, Scott reminds us of the early history of tobacco. Tobacco was nearly everywhere in the Americas, it is thought, by the time of Christ. An eleventh-century pottery vessel shows a Mayan man smoking a roll of tobacco leaves tied with a string—the Mayan term for smoking was *sik'ar* (to think that I have enjoyed cigars for years, and never realized the word was of Mayan origin!).

This gives rise to a general discussion of the history of tobacco. Columbus was given a gift of fruit and "certain dried leaves which gave off a distinct fragrance" by the natives when he first set foot in the New World. He ate the fruit, but having no idea of the leaves' use, he had them thrown overboard. A few years later, visiting Cuba and seeing the natives smoking, another explorer, Rodrigo de Jerez, brought the custom back to Spain—when his neighbors saw smoke billowing from his nose and mouth, they were so alarmed they called in the Inquisition, and Jerez was imprisoned for seven years. By the time he got out of prison, smoking had become a Spanish craze.

Then, of course, there were the stories we all learned as schoolchildren in England—of Sir Walter Raleigh introducing smoking in England (his alarmed servant, thinking his master was on fire, doused him with a jug of water); of tobacco getting honorable mention in *The Faerie Queene;* of the Elizabethans, with their pithiness, calling it sot-weed; and of Queen Elizabeth herself being inducted into smoking, as an old lady, in 1600. And then, in rapid succession, smoking was denounced in *Worke of Chimney Sweepers* (1601), defended in *A Defense of Tobacco* (1603), and reattacked (*A Counterblaste...*) by no less than King James himself. But despite royal disapproval and tariffs, by 1614 there were "7000 shops in and about London, that doth vent Tobacco." This gift from the New World was quickly adopted all over the Old.

By now we have arrived in the center of old Oaxaca, where the streets still run in the simple north-south grid laid out in the sixteenth century. Some of the streets, we notice, are named after political figures, like Porfirio Díaz Street, but others, to our pleasure, after various naturalists. I spot a Humboldt Street—Alexander von Humboldt, the great naturalist, visited Oaxaca in 1803 and described his experiences in his *Personal Narrative*. John Mickel points out a Conzatti Park. Conzatti, he says, was not a professional botanist—he was a school teacher and administrator who lived in Oaxaca during the 1920s and 1930s—but he was an amateur botanist, the first pteridologist in Mexico, who in 1939 documented more than six hundred Mexican fern species.

J.D., in the meantime, has spotted a tanager on a mango, and adds this to the list he is keeping.

We stop in the great colonial church of Santo Domingo. The church is enormous, dazzling, overwhelming in its baroque magnificence, not an inch free of gilt. A sense of power and wealth exudes from every inch of this church, a statement of the occupier's power and wealth. How much of the gold, I wonder, was mined by slaves, how much melted down from Aztec treasures by the conquistadors? How much misery, slavery, rage, death, went into the making of this magnificent church? And yet the statuary portrays smallish figures with dark complexions, as opposed to the idealized, enlarged statues of the Greeks. Clearly local models were used, and religious imagery adapted to local needs and forms. A giant golden tree emblazoned on the ceiling holds both court and ecclesiastical nobles in its branches—church and state mixed, as one.

A painting of the Virgin, gilded, ornate, blazes in the middle of the darkened, soaring nave ("Oh, my God," whispers J.D., "look at that!"). Below it a black-robed woman, perhaps a nun, is kneeling; she raises her voice intermittently in a loud, guttural song or invocation. She is in a state of ecstasy, adoration. I have the feeling of something theatrical, histrionic. If she wants to pray, I feel, let her do so discreetly, not make such a racket. Others, however, find her beautiful, moving.

Just outside the church, the street is lining with vendors selling hammocks, necklaces, wooden knives, paintings. I buy a many-colored hammock and a slender wooden knife. Scott does, too ("just to spread money around," he says). There are tiny shops across the street, and among them I notice Gastenterolia Endoscopica. I wonder, absurdly, why one should seek a colonoscopy, a gastroscopy, a sigmoidoscopy, in these holy confines?

Luis, our guide, is still plying us with information: "Here is the 'house of Cortés.' Cortés was never here, but he *would* have stayed here, lived here, had he ever visited Oaxaca. It is his *official* house." Next to the house, in the street, there is a truck full of gasoline, with Milleania Gas painted on the outside.

And in front of the church, this beautiful piece of architecture, is an unaccountably ugly garden—two large squares of reddish earth entirely planted with a treelike succulent, *Echeveria*—bizarre, spooky plants which look like triffids—*Echeveria,* and nothing else. There used to be a pleasant, variegated garden here, apparently, and then, by some perverseness, it was removed and replaced by this uncanny, red-earthed Martian plantscape.

A few blocks from Santo Domingo, we stop at a tiny but wonderful, aromatic spice shop. My botanical companions are fascinated, gastronomically, botanically. Scott tells me that there were at least a hundred and fifty plants domesticated before Columbus. We identify everything by its Latin name and its common name; everything is sniffed, olfactory nuances identified. Many of my companions buy exotic spices to take home; I content myself, timidly, with some pistachios and raisins.

There are huge, compacted towers of chilies, like bales, or castles—bright green, yellow, orange, scarlet, these seem very characteristic of Oaxaca. There are at least twenty types of chilies in common use—*chile de agua, chile poblano,* and *chile serrano* are the commonest fresh ones; there are also *chile amarillo, chile ancho, chile de arbol, chile chipotle, chile costeno, chile guajillo, chile morita, chile mulato, chile pasilla de Oaxaca, chile piquín* and a whole family of chilies going under the name of *chilhuacle*. I wonder whether these are all separate species, or varieties produced by domestication. All of them, presumably, differ in taste, in texture, in hotness, in complexity, in a dozen other dimensions to which the Oaxacan palate is sensitive—in New York I just have a bottle labeled Powdered Chili, and that has been the extent of my own sophistication so far.

Just across from the spice shop is a chocolate factory. We could smell it, the smell of roasting chocolate beans mixed with the scents of chilies and cinnamon, almonds, cloves, a block away. The factory has a tiny frontage on the street, but then one enters, from the dazzling sun, past the sacks of cocoa beans half-blocking the entrance, to an astonishingly deep and commodious space inside. One of my companions, Robbin Moran, begins to tell me of his experiences with cacao trees. A shy, unassuming man with horn-rimmed glasses who looks like a post-doc in his late twenties or thirties, Robbin is in fact a youthful forty-four, and like John, he is a curator of ferns at the NYBG.

Cacao trees have large glossy leaves, and their little flowers and great purplish pods grow directly from the stem. One can break open a pod to reveal the seeds, embedded in a white pulp. The seeds themselves, the cacao beans, are cream-colored when the pod is opened, but with exposure to air may turn lavender or purple. The pulp, though, has almost the consistency of ice cream, Robbin says, and a delicious, sweet taste. "Finding some cacao trees is one of the treats of being out collecting," he remarks. "You don't find a disused chocolate plantation every day, but there are plenty of them here in Mexico, in Ecuador and Venezuela, too." The sweet, mucilaginous pulp attracts wild animals, he adds. They eat the sweet pulp and discard the bitter seeds, which can then grow into new seedlings. Indeed, the tough pods do not open spontaneously, and would never be able to release their seeds, were it not for the animals attracted to their pulp. Early humans must have watched animals and then imitated them, Robbin speculates, opening the pods and enjoying the sweet pulp, as he does, whenever he comes across a cacao tree.

Over thousands of years, perhaps, early Mesoamericans had learned to value the beans as well, discovering that if they were scooped out of the pod with some pulp still attached, and left this way for a week or so, they would become less bitter as fermentation occurred. Then they could be dried and roasted to bring out the full chocolate flavor, much as we were seeing and smelling now.

The roasted beans, now a rich brown, are shelled and moved to a grinder—and here the final miracle happens, for what comes out of the grinder is not a powder, but a warm liquid, for the friction liquefies the cocoa butter, producing a rich chocolate liquor.

Attractive though it looks and smells, this liquor is scarcely drinkable, being intensely bitter. The Maya made a somewhat different version—their *choco haa* (bitter water) was a thick, cold, bitter liquid, for sugar was unknown to them—fortified with spices, corn meal, and sometimes chili. The Aztec, who called it *cacahuatl,* considered it to be the most nourishing and fortifying of drinks, one reserved for nobles and kings. They saw it as a food of the gods, and believed that the cacao tree originally grew only in Paradise, but was stolen and brought to mankind by their god Quetzalcoatl, who descended from heaven on a beam of the morning star, carrying a cacao tree. (In reality, Robbin says, it probably originated in the Amazon, like so many species; but we still remember this myth in the Latin name of the tree, *Theobroma,* "food of the gods.") The tree was rare at best, and now, he tells me, like the date palm and the avocado, it may be almost extinct in the wild.*

---

* It has been suggested by Connie Barlow, in her book *The Ghosts of Evolution,* that the near extinction of the wild avocado was caused by the disappearance twelve or thirteen thousand years ago of the giant *Toxodon* and other huge vegetarian mammals—giant ground sloths, glyptodonts, and gomphotheres—which were large enough to swallow the fruit and huge seed of the avocado whole, and then defecate the seeds in various parts of the forest. Now, with the extinction of the giant mammals, smaller animals, like the tapir, can only nibble round the seed and spit it out, denying it the distribution it needs. Basically it is human agriculture alone now, as with the date palm, that keeps the avocado alive. Ironically, it may also have been human intervention, in the form of hunting, that led to the extinction of the giant Pleistocene mammals.

It has been cultivated in Mexico, though, for more than two thousand years, and not only as a source of the divine drink—cacao pods served as symbols of fertility, often portrayed in sculptures and carvings, as well as a convenient currency (four cacao beans would buy a rabbit, ten a prostitute, one hundred a slave). Thus Columbus had brought cacao beans back to Ferdinand and Isabella as a curiosity, but had no idea of its special qualities as a drink.

Myth and legend seem to cluster round the history of cocoa. Legend asserts that Montezuma drank forty or fifty cups of the foaming chocolate daily, and that it was an aphrodisiac for him. Other legends claim that when Montezuma offered Cortés a cup of chocolate, Cortés was made dizzy by the bitter, chili-hot drink, but not so dizzy that he failed to notice that the cup was made of solid gold, and that Mexico must therefore be full of gold for the taking—or that the bitter drink, if sweetened, could enchant all of Europe, and constitute a profitable monopoly for Spain. The first cacao plantations, it is said, were planned by Cortés himself.

In the cacao shop, we are offered steaming cups of chocolate sweetened and spiced with almonds and cinnamon, the Oaxacan way. It is similar to the drink developed in the sixteenth century by the Spanish, who kept its complex refining process a secret for more than fifty years. But eventually the secret was out, and by the 1650s there were chocolate houses in Amsterdam and London, and soon throughout Europe (indeed, these preceded both teahouses and coffeehouses). The chocolate drink was a special hit at the French court, where its aphrodisiac qualities were highly esteemed—Madame de Pompadour mixed it with ambergris, Madame du Barry gave it to her lovers, and Goethe would travel nowhere without his own chocolate pot.

For Proust, a madeleine opened the gate of memory, evoking a world of private meanings and memories. But here, in this Oaxacan chocolate factory, the opposite has happened, in a sense: The gathered knowledge of chocolate—coming partly from my own reading, partly from Robbin, and partly from the proprietor himself—seems to pour itself into the cup of hot cocoa I am drinking, to give it a special dimension and depth.

But why, I wonder, should chocolate be so intensely and so universally desired? Why did it spread so rapidly over Europe, once the secret was out? Why is chocolate sold now on every street corner, included in army rations, taken to Antarctica and outer space? Why are there chocoholics in every culture? Is it the unique, special texture, the "mouth-feel" of chocolate, which melts at body temperature? Is it because of the mild stimulants, caffeine and theobromine, it contains? The cola nut and the guarana have more. Is it the phenylethylamine, mildly analeptic, euphoriant, supposedly aphrodisiac, which chocolate contains? Cheese and salami contain more of this. Is it because chocolate, with its anandamide, stimulates the brain's cannabinoid receptors? Or is it perhaps something quite other, something as yet unknown, which could provide vital clues to new aspects of brain chemistry, to say nothing of the esthetics of taste?

We return to our bus laden with chocolate and spices, and begin the journey back to our hotel. Since it is Saturday, a market day, we pause for a final stop at the main market, an entire city block filled with a warren of leather, textile, and clothing stalls.

Our group, of course, dallies by the fruits and vegetables, sampling them mentally and physically, moving from recondite botanical identifications and comparisons to ecstatic sighs (or occasional *eugghs!*) at their varied tastes. There are bananas with a huge range of colors and sizes—a tiny green one, unexpectedly, has the sweetest taste of all. There are oranges, limes, tangerines, and lemons, as well as pomelos, or shaddocks—the uncouth, pear-shaped wild ancestors of the grapefruit (its seeds, one of our group remarks, were originally brought back from Barbados by a Captain Shaddock in the seventeenth century). There are manzanitas, which look like loquats, but are not—Scott says they grow on a *Crataegus,* the Mexican hawthorn; he will point one out to me on one of our excursions.

There are sapotes, tennis-ball sized with shiny greenish-black skins. These are called date plums, says someone, and grow on a "marmalade tree." Wondering if I am having my leg pulled, I sink my teeth into the black flesh and find it as slimy as a persimmon, but with a taste nothing like dates, or plums, or marmalade, or persimmon. There are guavas and passion fruit and papayas, also juicy red cactus fruits of different sorts—some from the organ-pipe cactus, some from the prickly pear. The inside of the passion fruit looks like frog spawn or salamander eggs, but is, to my mind, the most delicious of all.

Vegetables too are immensely varied, with more varieties of beans than I have ever imagined, bringing home to me that beans, along with corn, are still the basic Mesoamerican food, as they have been since the dawn of agriculture here eight thousand years ago. Rich in protein, with amino acids complementary to those of corn—the two of them, together, supply all the amino acids one needs. We see chunks of white, chalky limestone everywhere, used for grinding with the corn, which makes its amino acids more digestible.* There are jicamas, with enormous, conical taproots that taste like water chestnuts and sweet peas. There are tomatoes of all sorts, but even more popular, tomatillos, husk-tomatoes, with green flesh and papery husks, used in making *salsa verde*. Tomatoes and tomatillos, I reflect, like "Indian corn," potatoes too, were also gifts of the New World to Europe. Nothing like them had ever been seen before. (Tomatoes, indeed, were regarded for many years with great suspicion, before people were persuaded that they were not poisonous. Like potatoes, they are in the Solanaceae family, a family full of particularly deadly plants, including the thorn apple and henbane. The tomato and potato are in fact members of the same genus as the deadly nightshade, and so, perhaps, some hesitation was understandable.)

And of course, being fern people, we cannot fail to notice certain ferns being sold for medicinal purposes—dried horsetails, used for treating blood diseases and as a diuretic; the rhizomes of rabbit's-foot ferns, *Phlebodium;* and the dried-up

---

* Robbin and I, sharing a fondness for fluorescent minerals, were curious about the limestone (we had seen the fluorescent calcite at the Franklin Mine in New Jersey), and we took a chunk of it back to the hotel with us, where we examined it under the ultraviolet light Robbin had brought with him. It was brilliantly fluorescent, and glowed a bright orange, like a glowing coal.

rosettes of the resurrection fern, which David had told me about in the airport—though what one did with these, no one seemed to know.

The beautiful white onions, the bananas, the flayed chickens, the hung meat...the sandals, the hats (I buy one, a splendid straw hat, a sombrero, for a dollar), the pottery, and mats. Above all, the human wonder. This market is so rich, so various, that, reluctantly, I put my notebook away. It would need more talent, more energy than I have, to begin to do justice to the phantasmagoric scenes here. And I hesitate to give offense, to seem an insensitive tourist.

I long for my camera, though photographing might be even more offensive (offense *has* been caused by outsiders, who will wander through the market buying nothing, but snapping whatever, whomever, they think cute or picturesque).

Back in the bus once again, I make a few brief notes: Pigs, of all sizes, tethered by their hind legs. Sheep, goats, flayed carcasses—stink! Goats by the dried-up river. Charcoal and wood sellers.

Bernal Díaz del Castillo marched with Cortés, and in his *True History of the Discovery and Conquest of New Spain* (which he wrote much later, as an old man), he described the great market near Tenochtitlán as he saw it in 1519. His list of its riches goes on for several pages, including in his "classes of merchandise" everything from stone knives to human slaves:

> Each kind of merchandise was kept by itself and had its fixed place marked out. Let us begin with the dealers in gold, silver,

and precious stones, feathers, mantles, and embroidered goods. Then there were other wares consisting of Indian slaves both men and women...and they brought them along tied to long poles, with collars round their necks so that they could not escape, and others they left free. Next there were other traders who sold great pieces of cloth and cotton, and articles of twisted thread, and there were *cacahuateros* who sold cacao....There were those who sold cloths of henequen and ropes and the sandals with which they are shod, which are made from the same plant, and sweet cooked roots and other tubers....In another part there were skins of tigers and lions, of otters and jackals, deer and other animals and badgers and mountain cats, some tanned and others untanned, and other classes of merchandise.

Díaz interrupts himself again and again to add something new, the scene of more than fifty years earlier still vivid in the mind of the now almost blind, old man in his eighties:

> ...beans and sage and other vegetables and herbs...fowls, cocks with wattles, rabbits, hares, deer, mallards, young dogs and other things of that sort...fruiterers...cooked food, dough and tripe...every sort of pottery made in a thousand different forms...honey and honey paste and other dainties like nut paste...lumber, boards, cradles, beams, blocks and benches... paper...tobacco, and yellow ointments...and much cochineal is sold under the arcades which are in that great market place....I am forgetting those who sell salt, and those who make the stone knives...gourds and gaily painted jars made of wood. I could wish that I had finished telling of all the

things which are sold there, but they are so numerous and of such different quality and the great market place with its surrounding arcades was so crowded with people, that one could not have been able to see and inquire about it all in two days.

CHAPTER THREE

SUNDAY

Today we will go on a botanical foray, over the mountains to the Llano de las Flores—"the meadow of flowers"— though now, in January, we are in the middle of the dry season, and there will be no flowers. The central hills and valley, indeed, are bone-dry, desertlike, brown. (It is difficult to imagine them otherwise, but I must return, I think, in the rainy season, when it is carpeted with *Rigidella*, an iris with brilliant scarlet flowers.)

We gather outside the hotel with gear of all shapes and sizes, for our high-altitude, perhaps wet trip—we will soon be at 9,000 feet or more. We have layered clothing, which we will doff, then don again, layer by layer, as we go from the tropical valley to near-freezing winter rain forest. We also bring collecting gear—mostly plastic bags for plant specimens (how different from the tin vasculums of my youth!)—as well as lenses, cameras, binoculars strung around necks. Several of us carry "the bible," the *Pteridophyte Flora of Oaxaca, Mexico.*

One young woman (she is from the local botanical garden) is carrying a plant press, and the sight of this raises questions about what one is allowed to collect. Collecting spores, we are assured, is fine. John speaks of ways of folding paper to enclose the spores—ways which are "seamless and seemly." "Don't use Scotch tape—the spores will stick to it!" he adds. But there are strict regulations about collecting anything else, and we do not have a license to bring plants back to the States. We may collect isolated fronds but no plants or seedlings, and we are encouraged to document everything photographically. (Almost everyone has macro lenses: I, foolishly, left mine in New York, but what I do have with me, which no one else has, is a stereo camera.)

And there is Dick Rauh, a botanical illustrator and teacher at the New York Botanical Garden, who will draw everything of interest—both the actual-size views and his beautiful, detailed enlargements, ten or fifteen times life-size. He carries sketch pad, pens, pencils, a medley of high-power lenses, and a pocket microscope.

Dick became a botanical illustrator only after retiring from a long, successful career as a designer of film credits, and is now nearing completion of a Ph.D. in botany, so he is quite knowledgeable about the plants he is drawing. I am fascinated by the relation of knowledge to perception, and ask him about this. I tell him of the amazing plant drawings I have seen by autistic savants—drawings based purely on perception, without any botanical knowledge. Dick, however, insists that knowledge and understanding only sharpen his perceptions, do not compromise them, so he now sees plants as more interesting and more beautiful, more miraculous, than ever before, and he can convey this, emphasize one aspect or another in a way which would be impossible in a literal drawing or in a photograph, impossible without knowledge and intention.

It will take two or three hours to reach the meadow—about eighty or ninety kilometers distant—with stops along the way. This part of our route, along the Pan American Highway, used to be, Luis says, an Aztec highway. But we turn off the Pan American Highway after a couple of kilometers, onto Highway 175, which goes from the Pacific Ocean to the Gulf of Mexico. At the junction is a statue of Benito Juárez, with panels around it showing episodes from his life. Luis promises to tell us all about him later—his tone is one of affection and reverence. He says that Juárez was born in the village of Guelatao, which we will be passing through.

We are now driving to the East Sierra Madre. I ask Scott about the many red flowers we pass. They are *Solanum,* he says. He tells me that some other species of *Solanum* are bat-dispersed and have greenish or white flowers, while these, bird-dispersed, have red flowers. The bat-dispersed ones waste no metabolic energy producing what would be, for them, a useless red pigment.

Scott and I speak of the coevolution of flowering plants and insects in the last hundred million years, the development of the dramatic colors and shapes and scents by which flowering plants lure insects and birds to their flowers. And we speak of how certain kinds of red and orange fruit seem to have appeared only in the last thirty million years or so, in tandem with the evolution of trichromatic vision in monkeys and apes (though birds had developed trichromatic vision long before). Such fruits, a staple of many monkey diets, were particularly visible to trichromatic eyes in the tangled jungle foliage, and the plants, in turn, relied on the monkeys to disperse their seeds in their feces.

The marvel of such coevolution, such mutual adaptation, is central to Scott's interests. He and his wife, Carol Gracie, together and separately, have spent their lives exploring it. But I, though I also appreciate the beauty of such adaptations, prefer the green and scentless world of ferns, an ancient green world, the world as it was before the coming of flowers. A world, too, with a charming modesty, where reproductive organs—stamens and pistils—are not thrust out flamboyantly but concealed, with a certain delicacy, on the undersides of leafy fronds.

Long after the sexuality of flowering plants was recognized, the reproduction of ferns remained a mystery. It was believed, Robbin told me, that ferns had seeds—how else could they reproduce?—but since no one could see these, they assumed an odd and almost magical status. Invisible themselves, they were thought to confer invisibility on others: "We have receipt of fern-seed, we walk invisible," says one of Falstaff's henchmen in *Henry IV*. The great Linnaeus himself, in the eighteenth century, did not know how ferns reproduced, and coined the term cryptogams to denote the hiddenness, the mystery, of their reproduction. It was only in the middle of the nineteenth century that it was discovered that in addition to the familiar fern plant with its spore-bearing fronds, the sporophyte, there also existed a tiny, heart-shaped plant, very easily overlooked, and that it was this, the gametophyte, which bore the actual sex organs. Thus there is an alternation of generations in ferns: Fern spores from the fronds, if they find a suitably moist and shaded habitat, develop into tiny gametophytes, and it is from these, when they are fertilized, that the new sporophyte, the baby sporeling, grows.

Most gametophytes, like liverworts, look much the same. The beauty of ferns, their enormous range of form, from towering tree ferns to tiny filmy ferns, from the delicately divided, lacy fronds to the thick, undivided leaves of staghorn and bird's-nest ferns—all this resides in the sporophyte form. And the sori themselves take on a variety of forms: whelks and bubicles in some species, creamy masses in others, and beautiful, fine parallel lines in bird's-nest ferns and others. Part of the joy of ferning is in turning over the fertile fronds and spotting these sporangia.

John Mickel loves the fertility, the sporangia of ferns. "Ooh!" he says of an *Elaphoglossum,* "isn't that nice, smeared sporangia on the other side." Of *Polystichum speciosissimum:* "Look at those scales and incurved margins!" And of a *Dryopteris,* which he has just found in the forest: "Fertile as a moose!" he says, gazing at its sporangia. John, Robbin whispers to me, jokingly, has "pteridological orgasms." I have often seen these at our Saturday fern meetings. His voice will rise, he will wave his arms about, use the most extravagant language (comparing spores, some-times, to caviar): "It makes one's heart go pit-a-pat."

··········

My own impulse, like John's, has always been to cryptogamic botany; I find flowers, with their explicitness, their floweriness, a little too much.

Indeed, many of us share this feeling, and when we have our AFS meetings on Saturdays, any mention of flowering plants tends to be accompanied by a sort of joking apology: "If you will excuse my mentioning it…" or "I know you won't like this, but…" You might think, hearing us on a Saturday morning, that we still lived in a flowerless, Paleozoic world, where insects play no role, and spores are dispersed by wind and water only. (I should add, in all fairness, that there is equally little reference among us to plants lower than ferns—mosses, liverworts, seaweeds, etc.—and I, with my predilection for the primitive fern allies and mosses, am sometimes, I imagine, suspected of apostasy.) Of course, the particular passion for ferns is embedded, in all of us, in a much broader botanical and ecological context— even the most ardent of fern systematists are aware of this—it is just that we pretend at times, in a sort of nostalgia or in-joke, to have no interest in the wider plant world.

Among my fern-loving fellow travelers, however, there are quite a few experts on flowering plants, too—J.D. and Scott among them—and now, on the bus, as we pass by some trees laden with glorious white flowers, Scott draws our attention to them. These, he says, are tree *Ipomoea*. *Ipomoea*, I query? The same genus as the morning glory? Yes, says Scott, the sweet potato, too. I think back to my California days, in the early 1960s, when morning glory seeds—one variety of them, at least (the "Heavenly Blue")—were used for their psychedelic power—since they contained ergot compounds, lysergic acid derivatives, similar to LSD. I used to get three or four packets of the hard, angular black seeds, pound them to powder with a mortar and pestle, then—this was my special innovation—mix the ground seeds with vanilla ice cream. There would be intense nausea for a while, followed by visions of a very personal heaven or hell. I often wished for the right place and time to take it—and this would have been in south Mexico, where the morning glory grows easily and abundantly in the mountains, and its seeds, *ololiuhqui,* can be kept indefinitely without losing their potency. Indeed, I am told, the plant itself (which the Aztec called *coatl-xoxo-uhqui,* green-snake, for its twining vine-like habit) was regarded as a sacramental plant, and used in the presence of a medicine man, a *curandero.*

In *Plants of the Gods,* the great ethnobotanist Richard Evans Schultes and the chemist Albert Hoffmann (who was the first to synthesize LSD and to report its effects), describe how every culture has discovered plants with hallucinogenic or intoxicant powers, powers often seen as supernatural or divine. But the Old World knew nothing like the powerful hallucinogenic drugs of Mexico—*ololiuhqui* (which the Spanish, when they encountered it, called *semilla de la Virgen,* seed of the Virgin); the sacred psilocybin mushroom, *teonanacatl,* God's flesh (its active constituents also lysergic acid derivatives); and in the north of Mexico, overlapping the southern U.S., the buds of *Lophophora williamsii,* the *peyotl* cactus, sometimes called mescal buttons (though these have nothing to do with mescal, the distilled liquor made from the agave plant).

As the bus churns up the mountain, Scott and I chat about these plants, and the more exotic South American hallucinogens, such as *ayahuasca* (the vine of the soul), made from the Amazonian vine *Banisteriopsis caapí,* which William Burroughs and Allen Ginsberg describe in *The Yage Letters;* and the tryptamine-rich snuffs—*Virola,* yopo, cojoba—the way in which their active ingredients are all so similar chemically, and so close in structure to serotonin, a neurotransmitter; and the way in which they were all discovered in prehistoric times (was it by accident, or trial and error?). We wonder why plants so different botanically should converge, so to speak, on such similar compounds, and what role such compounds play in the plant's life—are they mere by-products of metabolism (like the indigo found in so many plants); are they used (like strychnine or other bitter alkaloids) to deter or poison predators; or do they play some essential roles in the plants themselves?

It is extraordinary to sit next to Scott on the bus. He identifies, or can identify, everything we see, and he knows every plant in its meaning and context; the whole world of evolution, competition, adaptation, moves through his mind as we pass. I am reminded of another bus ride, in the state of Washington, with a friend from Guam, and how her knowledge of geology brought the entire inorganic landscape, all the landforms around us, as we passed them, to life. She, too, as it happens, was primarily a pteridologist, but her geological eye, so well-developed, gave an extra dimension, meaning, to everything we saw.

Accompanying us on the bus is Boone. I am not quite clear, at this point, as to who and what Boone is, though I know that he is an old and highly respected friend of John Mickel's—they met here in Oaxaca back in 1960—and that Boone has worked here as a botanist or agriculturist ever since. He has a house for visiting botanists, apparently, high up in the mountains, near Ixtlán, and we will be visiting this in a few days. Boone must be in his seventies; he is short but broad and strongly built, agile, and has a fine head with a cowlick of hair over his forehead.

He is evidently an expert on the trees of Oaxaca, and now, as we move higher into the mountains, and oaks and pines become the dominant vegetation, he gets up in the bus and starts to speak to us. "Most of the oaks," he starts, "are in such an active state of evolution that they cannot be identified. Some floras speak of thirty species, some of two hundred—and these hybridize constantly." The first pines we see have short needles and cones. Then, a few hundred feet higher up, pines with longer needles and larger cones, another species.

Clouds on the mountaintops—fabulous vista! As we climb a little higher, Boone points out a magnificent

Douglas fir on a precipitous outcropping to our left. This stand of Douglas firs was discovered, he adds, in 1994, by a botanist from the Hungarian Museum of Natural History. It is the southernmost population of Douglas firs in the world. Boone goes on to speak of Oaxaca as a uniquely rich botanical borderland where plants of northern origin, like these pines, mingle with South American plants that have migrated north.

Other plants: *Abies oaxacana*. Madrones—*Arbutus,* with red wood and peeling bark. Indian paintbrush, orange, along the road, admixed with blue lupins and a purple lobelia. Small yellow flowers—marigolds. Other yellow flowers are dismissed as DYCs—damned yellow composites. The plants of the Compositae family include dandelions, asters, thistles, and others, where the flower head is composed of florets radiating out from a central disc. They are among the most common of all wildflowers and often difficult to identify. Bird-watchers use similar phrases: There are fine, interesting birds, and then there are the LGBs—little gray birds— flitting everywhere, distracting the attention.

The bus climbs higher and higher, and now we get to the top of the ridge, 8,400 feet above sea level. A lumber road goes off to the left, up to the top of Cerro San Felipe. It is colder here, wetter, and more moss is to be seen. As we start our descent, we drive just a mile or two, and stop at a small gully called Río Frío. John Mickel immediately identifies a new fern, a spleenwort, *Asplenium hallbergii.* I ask, in an idiotic way, "Who was Hallberg?" John looks at me strangely, and says "Ask Boone!"

Then he swoops off to another fern, *Anogramma leptophylla.* "This is one of the great ferns of the world! It's full size, only an inch or two high. It's a cutie, only occurs at high elevations." He moves quickly to another fern, *Adiantum,* a maidenhair, and another, an *Asplenium.*

John becomes tremendously enthusiastic over almost every fern we see, and when he was asked which was his favorite, he had difficulty giving an answer. "When speaking on fern cultivation," he said, "I find myself citing the ostrich fern as my favorite, and a minute later the autumn fern is my favorite. In fact, I have three hundred favorite ferns. I love the ostrich fern for its great shuttlecock form and its wide-creeping runners, and the autumn fern for its red sori and dark lustrous fronds that remain standing upright and green all through the winter. I like the Himalayan maidenhair for its delicate beauty. Some of my favorites have special memories—I found the Mexican woodfern on top of Cerro San Felipe, here in Oaxaca, after its not having been collected anywhere for over a hundred years. For scientific study, *Anemia* and *Elaphoglossum* claim my vote, though *Cheilanthes* and *Selaginella* are close behind. How do you choose among your children? They are all wonderful, and the more you know them personally, the more you love them."

My attention wanders a bit—I see we are surrounded by sweet-smelling salvia, sage. And beautiful calla lilies in a field, in which there is a notice in Spanish which I puzzle out slowly: Anyone Who Does Not Respect This Property Will Be Jailed. Or shot, or beheaded, or castrated.

"Here's *Pleopeltis interjecta,*" John continues, "Big round sori with yellow spores," he says, looking at the clustered sporangia,

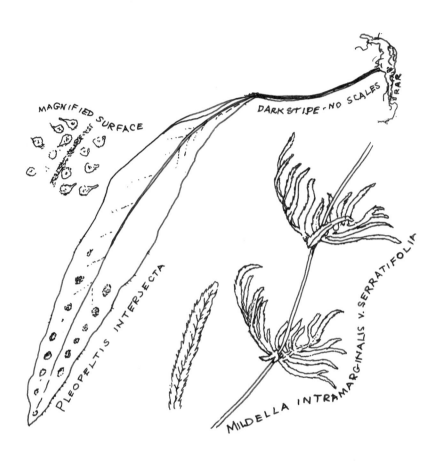

MAGNIFIED SURFACE

DARK STIPE - NO SCALES

RAR

PLEOPELTIS INTERJECTA

MILDELLA INTRAMARGINALIS V. SERRATIFOLIA

"a splendid specimen! Another *Mildella,* with smooth margins, *M. intramarginalis.* If it's serrate, it's *serratifolia.*" My head is spinning with all the different ferns and their names, and I move away and wander a bit by myself, homing in on a wonderful tree full of mosses and lichens. When ferns get too much for me, I need to go lower, to the simpler, less demanding forms. To appreciate this microworld one needs a powerful hand lens—we all carry these—or even (as Dick has) a pocket microscope, to see the tiny stars of mosses, the fairy cups of lichens.

I join Robbin, who is standing by a stream. He points out liverworts, and a hornwort, *Anthoceros,* in which one can see a blue-green, nitrogen-fixing bacterium, *Nostoc.* Animals, higher plants, even hornworts, he says, may think themselves superior, but ultimately we are all dependent on about a hundred species of bacteria, for only they know the secret of fixing the air's nitrogen so that we can build our proteins.

"Here's an *Elaphoglossum,* at last!" says John Mickel, climbing a crag. "There are six hundred species. They all look alike. This is..." He hems and haws, turning it this way and that under his lens. "This is *E. pringlei,* I guess."

Most ferns are fairly easy to distinguish and identify, by the size and form and color of their fronds, the way they are divided, their veins, the character and location of their sori, their general habitus. But *Elaphoglossum* is tricky in this regard. In his swift, minute, and almost intuitive examination, John must have looked at some very subtle differences, such as the form and distribution of the blade scales, characteristics visible only with a hand lens.

When I ask Boone about *Asplenium hallbergii* he is tactful enough to overlook my blunder, my failure to understand that *he* is Hallberg, that this is a species named in honor of him: Boone Hallberg. (I had failed to realize this, or forgotten it, because to everyone here, he is just "Boone.") I am intrigued by the mysterious Boone. I pick up fragments: He is not just a systematic botanist, Scott says. His interest has always been more in agriculture and ecology. He came to Mexico as a young man, drawn by the special needs of Oaxaca. He was especially concerned with deforestation, and tried hard to get people in different villages interested in the replanting of trees. He seemed to have a special gift for communicating with the local people directly and easily, getting things started from a grassroots level. He had been interested, too, in agricultural problems and possibilities, and especially the potentials of new sorts of corn.

Boone's Spanish seems as fluent and idiomatic as that of the local Oaxacans—he is earnestly conversing now with Fernando, the driver's son. Fernando is perhaps sixty years Boone's junior, but they are completely at ease with one another, the old man and the boy. Indeed, I get the sense that he is seen as something of a father figure by the local people.

I remember now—I failed to make the connection earlier—that Mickel and Beitel's book, the fern bible, is dedicated to Boone, for it was Boone who originally suggested to John that he catalog the ferns of Oaxaca. Oaxaca, he said, was probably richer in ferns than any other state in Mexico, and also among the least studied. Incited by Boone's suggestion, John had made a series of trips during the sixties and seventies, collecting nearly five thousand specimens from all over the state. Boone himself contributed another five hundred in the early seventies, many of them rarities. By 1988, when the *Flora* was published, John and his colleagues had discovered no fewer than sixty-five new species of fern, and catalogued a grand total of 690 species, in Oaxaca alone. Boone had been behind all this, providing room and board, guide service, logistical support and transportation.

Here in Mexico, Boone is saying, you have to use your brains to know what's going on. In the States everything is published, organized, known. Here it is under the surface, the mind is challenged all the while.

The richness of Oaxaca's ferns seems miraculous, for there are no more than a hundred or so in New England, perhaps four hundred species in the whole of North America. There are ferns in all latitudes—a brave thirty species in Greenland, for example—but far more as one goes toward the Equator. There are nearly 1,200 in Costa Rica, where Robbin teaches a course every year. And there is an incredible variety of shapes, sizes, formats, whole families of ferns with no exemplars in the temperate zones. In Oaxaca, too, there is every sort of habitat, from the arid central valley (itself a 5,000-foot-high plateau) to rain forest and cloud forest, to mountainsides. Tree ferns, climbing ferns, filmy ferns, shoestring ferns, they are all here, in unparalleled diversity.

Robbin's mind and mine, we discover, have both been going back to the little hornwort we had seen near the stream, with its precious, symbiotic freight of nitrogen-fixing bacteria. We are bathed in nitrogen, the atmosphere is four-fifths nitrogen. All of us, animals and plants and fungi alike, need it to manufacture nucleic and amino acids and peptides and proteins. But no organism other than bacteria can make use of it directly, so we are all dependent on these nitrogen-fixing bacteria to convert atmospheric nitrogen into forms of nitrogen the rest of us can use. Without this, life on Earth would not have got very far.

Intensive cultivation of a single crop tends to deplete the nitrogen in the soil quickly, but the Mesoamericans discovered early on, as other agricultural people did, by trial and error and experimentation, that beans or peas grown along with the corn could help replenish the soil more rapidly. (It was also discovered that alder trees, though not legumes, could similarly fertilize and enrich the soil, making possible a more intensive cultivation of other crops. The planting of alders had become an integral part of Mexican agriculture by 300 B.C.) In Europe, Robbin points out, many other legumes such as clover and alfalfa and lupin were grown as animal forage, and these were even more effective in restoring nitrogen to the soil than peas or beans. In China and Vietnam, he continues, warming to his theme, the great restorer is not a legume, not a flowering plant at all, but a tiny water fern, *Azolla,* which engulfs and lives with a nitrogen-fixing cyanobacterium, *Anabaena azollae.* Rice, half-submerged in rice paddies, grows much more vigorously if *Azolla* is ground into the mud—in Vietnam, they call this green manure.

Even though this practical knowledge had been around since the Stone Age, no one really knew why it worked, just that it did. Only in the nineteenth century was it realized that the strange nodules often present on the roots of legumes were full of bacteria, and that these, with their special enzymes, could fix atmospheric nitrogen and make it available to the plant (similarly with the nodules on alders, and the *Anabaena* in *Azolla*). With the eventual decomposition of such plants, the now-assimilable nitrogen compounds would be released into the soil.*

It was also realized around this time that however carefully one fertilized the soil with compost or with animal waste, however much one grew beans and vetches and clover and lupin, one could not feed an exploding human population without additional, inorganic fertilizers which were extremely nitrogen-rich. By the end of the nineteenth century, it was becoming clear that a nitrogen crisis was pending, that one had to have more ammonia or nitrates available if an exponentially expanding human population was not to starve—the catastrophe Malthus had dreamt of a century earlier. There was a rush on the South American beds of nitrates and guano (the Peruvians had long used these to guarantee a fertile soil), but these were exhausted in a few decades. Thus the supreme challenge, by the beginning of the twentieth century, was to make synthetic ammonia, for there was no longer enough natural fertilizer on the planet.

* Most of the world's plants—more than 90 percent of the known species—are connected by a vast subterranean network of fungal filaments, in a symbiotic association that goes back to the very origin of land plants, 400 million years ago. These fungal filaments are essential for the plants' well-being, acting as living conduits for the transmission of water and essential minerals (and perhaps also organic compounds) not only between the plants and fungi but from plant to plant. Without this "fragile gossamer-like net" of fungal filaments, David Wolfe writes in *Tales from the Underground,* "the towering redwoods, oaks, pines and eucalyptus of our forests would collapse during hard times." And so too would much of agriculture, for these fungal filaments often provide links between very different species—between legumes and cereals, for instance, or between alders and pines. Thus nitrogen-rich legumes and alders do not merely enrich the soil as they die and decompose, but can directly donate, through the fungal network, a good portion of their nitrogen to nearby plants. United by these multifarious underground channels (and also by the chemicals they secrete in the air to signal sexual readiness or news of predator attack, etc.), plants are not as solitary as one might imagine, but form complex, interactive, mutually supportive communities.

Now, of course, Robbin shrugs, the world is awash in synthetic fertilizers, and thousands of surplus tons of them drain into our lakes, rivers, and seas, disturbing the planet's nitrogen cycle and causing huge overgrowths of algae and whatnot. Not that this is any help, he adds, to a place like Oaxaca, which is much too poor to afford synthetic fertilizers anyhow. And this was where Boone came in—Boone, who saw, very clearly, from the first, that the farmers needed to be more productive, while remaining autonomous and independent of fertilizers from the U.S., and who wondered whether it might not be possible, by grafting or hybridization, to endow the cereals themselves with nitrogen-fixing bacteria.

Boone himself had found a very tall corn near the town of Totontepec, a corn whose roots had a slimy covering, and, examining this mucilage, he discovered that it contained several sorts of nitrogen-fixing bacteria. He had wondered whether it might be possible to get these bacteria into the corn itself, to breed, in effect, a nitrogen-fixing corn, and has been encouraging others to explore this. With genetic engineering, Robbin added, it might even be possible to bypass the bacteria and insert the gene for the nitrogen-fixing enzyme into the plants themselves.

Back in the bus, we are approaching El Cerezal ("the cherry orchard"), a little village, with no cherry trees that I can see, but pear trees blooming on the side of the road. We have to slow down, almost to a standstill, because of speed bumps (these are called "sleeping policemen") in the road. They were put here a few years ago, after a village girl was killed by a speeding bus. A hawk flying ahead of us, cries of excitement as it veers to one side of the bus.

I hear someone mutter, speaking of a certain group of ferns: "They're all pinnatifid." There is a huge amount of knowledge on this bus. It would be an irreparable loss to systematic botany, I think, if we crashed (as could easily happen, sliding into one of the sharp, precipitous ravines at every hairpin bend of the road).

Misted views of Ixtlán and Guelatao across the valley. Guelatao, Luis tells us, "is where Benito Juárez was born in 1806, the 21st of March. This is a holiday in Mexico." His life, his upbringing, his mission, is detailed by Luis. "He learned to read with the priests; went to the seminary; met there with philosophers; he took from there some of the ideas and maxims he used in his presidency. Then he went to the University of Oaxaca to become a lawyer. Became the governor of Oaxaca—and finally the president of Mexico, in 1856." We are treated to an elaborate discourse on the situation and politics of Mexico in 1856. A polite and finally stupefied silence greets this. Meanwhile, all sorts of wonderful plants slide past us.

Church property annexed by the government, its taxes went to the State, its controls and powers also. This reform led to the French invasion. Luis's voice continues as a background, while I gaze through the window at the village of San Miguel del Río across the valley. Huge bald cypresses, *Taxodium,* edge the river there.

We are descending now, from a high ridge, into the valley of the Río Grande. "If I can interrupt," says Boone, getting to his feet (no one else would have had the temerity to interrupt

Luis's dissertation on Mexican history), "We would now be crossing this old steel bridge, which was built in 1898 by the Cleveland Corporation, but sadly, last year, it was destroyed by a dump truck." The bridge, one end demolished, lies obliquely, half-submerged in the water. J.D., more attuned to birds than the destruction of old things, spots a gray silken flycatcher on one of its posts.

Extraordinary that a man, a Zapotec, from a small village, Luis continues, could become the president of Mexico. With his humble origins, his feeling for poor people, his liberal ideas, he was the Abraham Lincoln of Mexico. Luis goes on to tell us stories, myths, of Benito Juárez's childhood, little stories which showed his character, pointed to his future greatness and destiny.

Now the bus has climbed again, almost two thousand feet, and we can see the village of Ixtlán uphill to the right. Boone points to his home and botanical station high on a cloud-capped ridge overlooking Guelatao. For about a mile now, he says, there is a new dominant *Civocarpus,* something *macrophylla.* (What is a *Civocarpus,* I wonder?)[*] He knows every turn and twist of the road, every square mile, of this wild and beautiful country.

I wonder what his story is, what motivated him to come here, as a young man, in the 1940's.

I get talking with Scott about our primordial need to identify, to categorize, to organize. He himself, he says, rather than spotting species, immediately goes to a wider category—the family—and then homes in to genus and species. How much, we wonder, is such categorizing hard-

---

[*] I must have misheard the name, for when I asked the others later what "Civocarpus" was, none of them had the foggiest idea.

wired in the brain? How much learned? Is "animate/inanimate," for example, a hardwired category? Or the reaction of primates to snakes? Must baby bats and baby birds be taught their pollination targets? We speak of birdsong, half-wired, half-learned.

Finally we arrive at the Llano de las Flores. John Mickel moves about swiftly, identifying all the ferns: shield ferns, holly ferns, lady ferns, fragile ferns, bracken, sometimes fifteen feet high—all common in temperate regions. And *Plecosorus speciosissimus* and *Plagiogyria pectinata*. I love these rolling, Latinate names, redolent of a long-past scholastic age. Clubmosses, lilliputian plants out of fairyland with tiny leaves and cones, clothe the sides of the ravine. There are also many epiphytes, wreathing the trunks of trees, leaving scarcely an inch uncovered. Usually these epiphytes are harmless, clinging to the bark of trees without parasitizing or hurting them—unless the sheer weight of the epiphytes brings the tree down. (I have heard of this happening in the Australian rain forest, where staghorn ferns may weigh a monstrous five hundred pounds or more.)

J.D., off in the bracken, is in ornithological ecstasy, his bulky bearded figure jerks this way and that, as he spots new species, new varieties. Exclamations of delight burst continually from his lips. "My God! My God! Look at that...so beautiful..." His enthusiasm, his lyricism, never wanes, his sense of the birds' beauty and freshness. He is like Adam in the garden of Eden.

I am fond of bracken, or brake, I confess, partly because the old names excite me. There are fourteenth-century manuscripts that speak of "braken & erbes," and the name survives in many Germanic languages, including Norwegian and Icelandic. It is a pleasure to look at, with its solitary spreading frond, light green in the spring, darkening later, sometimes covering sunny hillsides. If one is camping out, it is comfortable to sleep on, better than straw, because it absorbs and insulates so well. But it is one thing to sleep on it, admire it, and quite another to eat it, as cattle and horses sometimes do when the tender young shoots come up in spring. Animals that eat bracken may develop the "bracken-staggers," because bracken contains an enzyme, thiaminase, which destroys the thiamine necessary for normal conduction in the nervous system. As a neurologist, this intrigues me, for such animals may lose their coordination and stagger, or show "nervousness" or tremor, and if they continue to eat the bracken, they will get convulsions and die.

But this, I now find, is only a tiny part of bracken's repertoire. Robbin calls bracken "the Lucrezia Borgia of the fern world," for it packs a series of horrors for the insects that eat it. The young fronds release hydrogen cyanide as soon as the insect's mandible tears into them, and if this does not kill or deter the bug, a much crueler poison lies in store. Brackens, more than any other plant, are loaded with hormones called ecdysones, and when these are ingested by insects, they cause uncontrollable molting. In effect, as Robbin puts it, the insect has eaten its last supper. The Romans used to cover their stable floors with a litter composed mostly of bracken. In one such stable, dating from the first century, 250,000 puparia of the stable fly were found, almost all showing arrested or perverted development.

And—as if all this were not enough—bracken also contains a powerful carcinogen, and though cooking destroys most of the bitter tannins and the thiaminase, humans who consume large quantities of bracken fiddleheads over long periods are more apt to develop stomach cancers. With this fearful chemical arsenal, and its aggressively spreading, almost unkillable, deep-underground rhizomes, bracken is potentially a monster, capable of carpeting huge areas of ground and depriving all the other ground-cover plants of sunlight.

But the bracken here, *Pteridium feei,* is gorgeous, and—unlike the common brackens—it is quite rare and special, an endemic species confined to southern Mexico, Guatemala, and Honduras.

Tomorrow, on the Atlantic slope, John promises, we will see a species of *Pteris*—a generic name confusingly similar to *Pteridium,* but a quite distinct genus and family; we will see the magnificent *Pteris podophylla,* which has most unusually constructed fan-shaped fronds ten or twelve feet in length. John has been effusive, almost lyrical, about its giant "pedate" fronds, so I decide to read up on it in his *Flora.* But looking up *P. podophylla,* I get waylaid by a description of another *Pteris, P. erosa,* which John and his colleague Joseph Beitel discovered on their Oaxaca expedition in 1971. What astounds me most here, is to see that their description in English is preceded by a paragraph in Latin: "*Indusio fimbrato, rachidis aristis 1 mm longis necnon frondis dentibus marginalibus apicem versus incurvis diagnoscenda.*" When I ask John about this, he explains that whenever a new species is discovered or claimed, its formal description, its diagnostic criteria, has to be, by tradition, in Latin. I knew that this had been the case centuries ago, in zoology and mineralogy as well as botany—but only in botany has this strange, medieval habit persisted.

Having ferned for an hour, we take a break for our lunch and I eat, unwisely, quite an enormous meal (the altitude—we are at 9,000 feet—has given me an appetite). A sandwich, two sandwiches, a third sandwich, dessert, and a couple of beers to top it off. Then we troop back into our bus and backtrack, just a couple of miles to a side road. This little road, John tells us, is exceedingly beautiful, passing through an epiphyte-hung forest to a limestone outcropping with a great range of ferns. We start walking briskly along the road, which winds up to almost 10,000 feet—too briskly for me, I start to realize, because I have begun to feel rather ill. My large meal, the gaseous beer, has blown up inside me, and as the road climbs I feel short of breath. My heart is thumping, a wave of nausea comes over me, I break out into a cold sweat. Altitude sickness, plus the folly of a large meal. "Take it easy!" someone remarks as they stride past me. I may be reasonably fit, I think, but I am sixty-six years old, and not yet accommodated to this altitude. I have a sense that the blood is draining from my head, and that my face, if there were anyone to see it, has gone quite gray. I would like to stop and rest, but feel I must hurry to keep up with the others. The nausea grows worse, my head pounds, I start to feel dizzy. Part of me says it is nothing, it will pass; but another part of me is becoming intensely anxious, and suddenly I am convinced that I may die here and now, so I sit down abruptly on a boulder, panting for breath, no energy even for making notes. I will reconstruct the afternoon's activities when I return to the hotel this evening.

CHAPTER FOUR

MONDAY

An early morning walk near our hotel with Dick Rauh and his wife went astray this morning. We got lost, and almost killed, trying to cross the Pan American Highway. We saw open sewers, children with infected eyes and sores. Fearful poverty, filth. We were almost asphyxiated by diesel fumes; we were almost bitten by a ferocious, perhaps rabid dog. This is the other side of Oaxaca, a modern city, full of traffic, with a rush hour, and poverty, like any other. Perhaps it is salutary for me to see this other side, before I get too lyrical about this Eden.

I have wanted to see the famous Tule tree, El Gigante, the colossal bald cypress in the churchyard of Santa María del Tule, for fifty or more years, ever since seeing an old photo of it in Strasburger's *Textbook of Botany* in my biology days at school, trees. *Taxodium distichum* is a deciduous tree, forming extended swampy woods on the north coast of the Gulf of Mexico from Florida to Galveston; the short shoots have two ranks of leaves and are shed as a whole. *T. mexicanum* is evergreen and is widely distributed on the highlands of Mexico; very large

Fig. 624.—*Taxodium mexicanum* in the churchyard of S. Maria de Tule at Oaxaka. This giant tree is one of the oldest living. (From a photograph.)

specimens occur, such as the giant tree of Tule, which at a height of 50 m. was 44 m. in circumference, and was estimated by von Humboldt to be 4000 years old (Fig. 624).

and reading that Alexander von Humboldt, who visited it in 1803, thought it might be four thousand years old. The notion that Humboldt himself made a special journey to see it, that I am now standing, almost two hundred years later, where he might have stood, adds a special dimension. Humboldt is a great hero of mine, and has been since I was fourteen or fifteen. I love his enormous, insatiable curiosity, his sensitivity and boldness—he was the first European to climb Chimborazo, Ecuador's highest Andean peak, and thought nothing, in his late sixties, of embarking on a wild journey through Siberia, collecting minerals and plants, making meteorological observations. Not only did he have this manifest feeling for the natural world, but he was also, it seemed (this is not so of all naturalists or even anthropologists) unusually sensitive to the different cultures and peoples he encountered.

Though we are still on the outskirts of the city of Oaxaca, in Humboldt's day, I imagine, this church and its tree were very isolated. One sees this plainly in the old photo, where the church is surrounded by open countryside, whereas now there is a bustling village all around it—indeed, it has almost been absorbed into the city itself.

The tree is too big for the eye to take in fully. It must have seemed even more extraordinary before the mission and town were built. It dwarfs the mission, makes it look like a toy. Not just its height (a mere 150 feet), but its girth (almost 200 feet around the trunk), and the far huger foliage, which, mushroomlike, tops the monstrous trunk.

A world of birds fly in and out—they have their residences, their apartments, in the tree. Scott pulls out his hand lens and camera, carefully examines and photographs the cones—the female ones at eye-level, the males higher up.

Takashi Hoshizaki, lean and agile for all his seventy-five years, and wearing a badge-filled green felt hat, compares the Tule tree with the bristlecones in California, said to be six thousand years old. I mention the famous Dragon Tree of Laguna in the Canary Islands, also reputed to be six thousand years old, a tree which led Humboldt to such lyrical extravagances that Darwin himself was deeply disappointed when, due to a quarantine, he was unable to see it. Two thousand years ago, Takashi tells me, this whole area was lush, embedded in a swamp; now it is arid, semidesert for much of the year, and only the Tule tree, with its vast roots and great age, survives to tell the tale. What else, I wonder, has El Gigante seen? The rise and fall of half a dozen civilizations, the coming of the Spaniards, the whole human history of Oaxaca.

··········

Luis is telling us the prehistory of Oaxaca, stimulated, perhaps, by the great age of the Tule tree: Asian peoples crossing the Bering Strait around 15,000 B.C., in the last ice age, then moving down through North America—hunting game, fishing, and gathering. Then, a few thousand years later, the woolly mammoths, the mastodons, the great mammals die. Did human hunting play a part here? Was it natural disaster, or climatic change? The hunter-gatherers, perforce, sought other modes of survival, and learned to cultivate maize, beans, squash, chilies, and avocados (still, today, the basic crops of Oaxaca). By 2000 B.C., as one historian writes, "Mesoamerica was a farmer's world, with agricultural villages scattered through the highlands and the lowlands."

Luis speaks of the establishment of permanent village settlements, clustered in areas of prime agricultural land—villages distinguished, very early, by particular customs, skills, and tongues. We know what the villagers ate, he continued, from the remains—corns and beans, avocados, chilies, supplemented by a certain amount of deer and peccary, wild turkey, and other birds. We know that dogs were domesticated, but nonetheless eaten. We know that the men wore loincloths and sandals, the women cloth or fiber skirts. We know that travel and trade was established very early (villages in Oaxaca had obsidian from central Mexico or Guatemala, hundreds of kilometers away, perhaps as early as 5000 B.C.), and that religion and ritual played a major part in their lives.

Between 1000 and 500 B.C., the first large cities were established, with a monumental architecture, and a new level of art and ritual, of social complexity, of writing. The largest of these cities was Monte Albán, which we would see for ourselves on Friday. It was under the Zapotec that Monte Albán reached its highest development, ruling a large region and prospering for fifteen hundred years. For unknown reasons, this great city was suddenly abandoned around A.D. 800, and there arose in its stead a series of smaller, provincial capitals. Yagul, which we were on our way to see, had been such a capital; Mitla, which we would see on Thursday, was another. These smaller centers carried on the Zapotec culture, variously enriched by other cultures in turn: the Mixtec, from western Oaxaca, around A.D. 1100, then the Aztec, from the north, around 1400. A hundred years later, Luis concluded, the Spanish came, and did all they could to obliterate everything which had gone before them.

As we approach Yagul, Luis points out a cliff face with a huge pictograph painted in white over a red background, an abstract design; and above it, a giant stick figure, a man. It looks remarkably fresh, almost new—who would guess it was a thousand years old? I wonder what the image means: Was it an icon, a religious symbol of some kind? A warning to evil spirits, or invaders, to keep away? A giant road sign, perhaps, to orient travelers on their way to Yagul? Or a pure, for-the-love-of-it pictographic doodle, a prehistoric piece of graffiti?

Entering Yagul, I see nothing at first, except grassy mounds and piled-up stones, vague, blurred, meaningless, flat—but bit by bit, as I look and listen to Luis, it starts to come into focus. Robbin picks up a broken potsherd, and wonders how old it is. These gentle ruins do not seem too dramatic at first—it takes a special eye, an archaeological eye, a knowledge of history, to clothe them with the significance they have, to imagine the past cultures which lived and built here. One can see a central grassy courtyard with central altar and platform around it, oriented, Luis tells us, northwest to southeast. Did the Zapotec have compasses, or did they reckon from the sun?

Four grass-covered mounds surround the altar; one of them has been opened to give access to the tomb below. I descend fearfully—it is surprisingly chilly, almost icy, ten feet down, and a fear of being buried alive suddenly seizes me. Listening to Luis, I have a vision of young men, captured warriors, being sacrificed on the altar, their torsos sliced open with obsidian knives, their hearts torn out and offered to the gods. Reemerging, dazzled, into the midday sun, I can now see the remnants of what was once a great palace, with labyrinthine passages and patios and little rooms—at least, the ground plan of a palace, for most of the stones have disappeared.

I am starting to get a sense of a life, a culture, profoundly different from my own. The feelings are similar, in some ways, to those one has in Rome or Athens, but quite different in other ways, because this culture is so different: so completely sun-oriented, sky-oriented, wind- and weather-oriented, as a start. The buildings face outward, life faces outward, whereas in Greece and Rome the focus is inward: the atrium, the inner rooms, the tabernacles, the hearth. What sort of poems and epics did these Mesoamerican civilizations produce? Were they ever recorded, or did they remain spoken only?

Yagul is our first intimation of what Mesoamerica might have been like, the cultures that lived here a thousand, two thousand years ago. But this, Luis says, is only a prelude; we will see much more spectacular ruins later in the week.

A lethargic dog lies on a step in the shade. I sit down next to it—it opens a lazy eye and scans me, then, seeing I am no menace, indeed a sort of brother, it closes it and we sit together in peace. I feel our rapport, the flow of feeling between us. It is resting, but, at the same time, ready—like a lion with half-closed eyes on the veldt; or a crocodile, motionless, awaiting unwary prey, able to explode into full activity in an instant. What is the physiology of this resting-ready state, and do we, human beings, employ it as well?

Yagul having been dutifully traversed, our botanists scatter in the fields outside and climb up the hill overlooking Yagul, looking at the dried-up ferns of this bone-dry terrain. Dried-up, but far from dead (although to me, to an ignorant eye, the ferns look as withered, as dead as any plants are likely to be)— in this state, their metabolism is almost zero. But let them get a night of rain, John Mickel tells us, or put them overnight in water, and the next morning they will have expanded and come alive, beautifully fresh and green.

The most fascinating to me is the so-called resurrection fern (actually a fern ally), *Selaginella lepidophylla,* which, I now remember, I had seen as tight brown rosettes in the market. We gather some rosettes to put in water overnight.

It takes a practiced eye to see dried-up, withered, and contracted ferns, to pick them out from the brown earth about them, but most of the group have had experience with this, and now, lenses in hand, careless of their clothes, they are crawling all over the ground, climbing the slopes, picking out new ferns every second. "*Notholaena galeottii!*" someone cries. "*Astrolepis sinuata!*" cries another, and there are no fewer than five species of *Cheilanthes.* These, however, are the most difficult to find because they have shed their fronds to minimize water loss, and are reduced to an almost featureless brown stalk. The stalks look dead, but will come to, John says, within hours of the first rainfall in spring. Like the resurrection fern, these plants have adapted brilliantly to life in the desert—in this case with a special abscission layer on the stem which allows the plant to quickly shed its fronds to reduce evaporation.

Almost the only green in this parched landscape comes from the bunches of mistletoe tapped into the vascular systems of some of the trees—unwilling hosts (I imagine), for though the mistletoe provides some of its own nourishment through photosynthesis (it is only a "semiparasite," Robbin tells me), it seems to rob its host of both water and nutrients—the branches distal to them look thin and attenuated. These monstrous bunches of mistletoe make me shudder inside, as I think of them settling on, draining, killing, their host trees. I think of other forms of parasites, and of psychological parasites—and how people can live on, parasitize, and ultimately kill others.

I strike up a conversation with David Emory, a great enthusiast (always the first to leap out of the bus for all his unwieldy-seeming bulk, to lie flat on the ground, bend double, scramble up slopes, to find plants). David was a chemistry teacher in his youth (now he teaches biology), and we begin swapping chemical stories and memories—his memory of a mercury hammer (the mercury frozen in alcohol and dry ice), and of putting ferric chloride on both sides of a hand, then adding X to one side, and Y to the other, which then turned them red and blue. What are X and Y, he asks me? Y, I say, is potassium ferrocyanide, turning the ferric chloride to Prussian blue. I hesitate about the red—it is potassium thiocyanate, he tells me. "Of course!" I say, angry with myself, and the cherry-red of ferric thiocyanate instantly comes back to me.

David liked my *New Yorker* piece, my memories of "a chemical boyhood," liked my reference to orpiment and realgar, the euphonious sulfides of arsenic, and says that *his* favorite arsenic sulfide was the strangely named "mispickel," which his students always took for the name of a sour maiden lady, Miss Pickle. Thereafter, whenever David and I meet, we have a three-part greeting consisting of these sulfides. He says "Orpiment," to which I retort, "Realgar," and he caps the trio with "Mispickel!"

CHAPTER FIVE

TUESDAY

7 a.m.: Sunrise over the hills. I sit here alone, the hotel dining room strangely empty and silent. The group left at five o'clock this morning for a sixteen-hour trip over the mountains, over the 10,000-foot pass, to the Atlantic slope with its unique ferns—its tree-ferns!—on the other side. With mixed feelings I excused myself from this—ten hours in a jolting bus would excruciate my back. The walking, the plant-hunting, the sense of exploration I love, but long sitting in a bus, anywhere, becomes an ordeal. So I will take a quiet day off for myself—lounge, read, swim, ponder what I am doing, what it all comes down to. I will spend a few hours in the central plaza in town, the *zócalo*—we had just a glimpse of it on Saturday, and it filled me with longing.

I have found a little table at an outdoor cafe in the zócalo. The cathedral, noble, dilapidated, is to my left, and this charming, alive plaza is full of handsome young people and cafés. In front of me old Indian women in serapes and straw hats sell religious icons and trinkets by the cathedral. The trees (Indian laurels, so-called, though they are a species of fig) are verdant, and the sky and air springlike. Huge clusters of balloons, helium-filled, strain upward on their leashes—some look big enough to carry a child away. Some have broken free and have lodged in the branches of trees above the square. (Some, too, it occurs to me, ascending to an immense height, may enter the intakes of jet engines and bring them flaming to the ground—I have a sudden vivid image of this, but it is an absurd thought.)

Tourists, pale-faced, awkward, uncouthly dressed, instantly stand out from the graceful indigenes. I am offered a souvenir, a wooden comb, as I sit, my own tourist pallor, and alienness, no doubt equally conspicuous.

Writing, like this, at a café table, in a sweet outdoor square...this is la dolce vita. It evokes images of Hemingway and Joyce, expatriate writers at tables in Havana and Paris. Auden, by contrast, would always write in a secluded, darkened room, curtained against the outside world and its distractions. (A young man with a placard parades in front of me: Confess Your Sins! Or Jesus Cannot Save!) I am the opposite. I love to write in an open sunny place, the windows admitting every sight and sound and smell of the outside world. I like to write at café tables, where I can see (though at a distance) society before me.

I find eating, and movement, most conducive to writing. My favorite environment, perhaps, is a dining car on a train. It was in such a dining car, supposedly, that the physicist Hans Bethe conceived the thermonuclear cycle of the sun.

The balloon seller, holding her gigantic mass of balloons, crosses the cobbles in front of me to put something in a trash can. Her gait is extraordinarily light, almost floating. Is she, in fact, half-levitated by the helium?

A charming gazebo with a cupola and dome, and delicate metal fretwork, stands in the middle of the square. (Later, to my surprise, I found I could descend beneath the cupola, to half a dozen subterranean, polygonal shops—a beehive of hexagonal units.) It looks, actually, a bit like a spaceship—like the alien ships in the film version of *The War of the Worlds*.

I love these little sketches, impressions. I am tired of the labor, the endlessness, of my chemical book! Perhaps I should stick to little narratives and essays, feuilletons, footnotes, asides, aperçus....

I am left alone, even treated (I fancy) with a certain respect, perhaps with my bulk, my incessant pen, and my beard, I am seen as a sort of Papa Hemingway figure.

A man, hung with a frame containing tiny cages of birds.

Children come up to me as I write. *"Peso, peso..."* Alas, (or perhaps fortunately), I have none, at least no coins. I spent my last five pesos on a loaf of bread at the market—a penny loaf. It was much larger than I realized, though beautifully light. It took me a sustained twenty minutes to eat it.

It is one o'clock now—the day, quite chilly at seven a.m., has become rather warm. When I came to this square a few hours ago, everyone avoided the shade and sat huddled in the sun, warming themselves like lizards in its rays; now the pattern is reversed—the sun-baked cafés and benches are deserted, while those in the cool shade are packed. And then, in the late afternoon, they trek back to catch the sun's last rays. It would be nice to have a time-lapse film of this diurnal migration. A frame every thirty seconds, a thousand in eight hours, would give a delightful minute-long summary of this cycle.

The young evangelist, with his placards from Corinthians 5:7, stands where he was before, impervious to the outer world, these secular fluctuations. His mind is fixed on the Kingdom of Heaven.

An armored car sits by the side of the plaza opposite the bus stop. A heavy bag (of bullion?) is transferred from hand to hand into the truck by two uniformed guards. Another officer covers the guards with a very efficient-looking automatic. It is all over within thirty seconds.

The hotel bus shuttles me back, along with a cigar-smoking man and his wife, who are speaking Swiss German. The conjunction of hotel shuttle and language takes me back, suddenly, to 1946—the war had just ended, and my parents decided to visit Europe's only "unspoiled" country, Switzerland. The Schweizerhof in Lucerne had a tall, silent electric brougham which had been running quietly and beautifully since it was made, forty years earlier. A sudden half-sweet, half-painful memory comes up of my thirteen-year-old self on the verge of adolescence. The freshness and sharpness of all my perceptions then. And my parents—young, vigorous, just fifty. Would I have wanted, had it been offered to me, a foreknowledge of the future?

··········

When I arrive back at the hotel, I see the participants of an International Conference on Low-Dimensional Physics—they too are here in the hotel, having their formal meetings every morning. What do they talk about, I wonder? Flat explosions, a Flatland world? There has been no contact between us and them—the world *we* call "real," our pteridological world, is doubtless too coarse for them, and theirs, perhaps, too subtle for us. Yesterday I overheard someone say "You mean to tell me these ordinary-looking people are theoretical physicists!" (Theoretical physicists, I once read, lead all scientists in intelligence, with an average IQ in excess of 160.) Observing some of them today, I am not sure they do look "ordinary." I see (or imagine) piercing intelligence animating their voices and gestures, but I could well be mistaken. I am not sure whether the super-intelligent scientists I know exhibit any external signs of their great gifts. And I remember contemporary descriptions of Hume—that he resembled "a turtle-eating alderman," that his own mother thought him "weak-minded," and that the salons of Paris were bewildered, and intrigued, by the total disparity of inner and outer man. There are similar descriptions of Coleridge's face: pudding-like, jowly, inexpressive, much of the time, but transformed, transfigured, by the vitality of his mind.

I sometimes think I have rather a stupid face myself, though most people seem to feel it is a kindly one. This, too, is my own impression when (as happens not infrequently) I fail to recognize myself in unexpected mirrors and windows and think, "Who is that amiable, kindly old fool?" But I have also caught looks of intense concentration, sudden animations of joy or inspiration, and looks of piercing sorrow and desolation, rage too, so it cannot be as pudding-like, as inexpressive, as I fancy.

I swim after my day sitting and walking in the city. The hotel has a beautiful pool, but I cannot sprint-swim very far at this altitude. Now a meal in the restaurant by myself—the place is almost empty, for our group is still on its daylong trip, and the high-IQ physicists are having a two-dimensional meal, no doubt, somewhere in town.

I find myself thinking of Scott, who told me yesterday that his true desire is to produce a beautiful botany book with rich, comprehensive texts and lovely, accurate illustrations. He hopes that the atlas he has been working on for ten years—of all the vascular plants of central French Guiana, the flowers, all their forms, colors, aromas—will be a book of such value and beauty. He is ambitious, he allows, for a beautiful botany book, but he has no sense of professional rivalry or competition. When I relayed these comments to a colleague, he was surprised. But perhaps he knows only the outer Scott, the administrator, the head of a busy department. For while Scott may be, may have to be, "a tough nut" outside, in order to keep his department going at a time when field botany is giving way to genomics and lab science—there must be another Scott as well, more inward, more lyrical, more concerned with the Ideal, and it is this Scott who dreams of "a beautiful book."

The fern tour is turning out to be much more than a fern tour. It is a visit to another, a very other, culture and place; and (so saturated is everything, everyone, here in the past) it is as much a visit, in a profound sense, to another time. The fusion of cultures hits one everywhere—in the faces, in the language, in the art and pottery, the mixed, colorful styles of architecture and dress, the complex doubleness of the "colonial" at every point. Luis, our guide, though Hispanic in many ways, also has the dark skin, the powerful build, the high cheekbones of a Zapotec. His ancestors, some of them, crossed the Bering Strait in the last ice age; B.C., for these people, means Before Cortés, the absolute divide between the pre-Conquest, the pre-Hispanic—and what happened later.

CHAPTER SIX

WEDNESDAY

I more and more regret that I did not go on yesterday's marathon trip to the rain forest, for everyone is telling me of its wonders, and some of these will be displayed at a show-and-tell this afternoon. How could I have sacrificed this to the banality of a slipped disk? After yesterday's long and exhausting day, today is one for "optional activities," and the most attractive one of these, to my mineral-loving mind, is a visit to the Hierve el Agua mineral springs.

The area itself is fairly arid, only two hours away from Oaxaca city, and we will be able to see some unusual stunted palms (they grow in clusters, resembling, says my *Oaxaca Handbook,* in an unusual burst of imagery, "regiments of desert dwarfs"). We will see more xerophytic ferns, adapted to the dryness—these never cease to fascinate me, because I always used to think of ferns as water-loving, shade-loving, delicate, vulnerable; and here one sees ferns able to survive blistering sun and prolonged dryness almost as well as euphorbs or cacti. And, I am told, there is a great variety of other plants—and birds—too, and it is this which animates J.D., who has also come along.

J.D. gets extremely excited at seeing a rare specimen which he has never seen before. Though he works at the New York Botanical Garden, he is not primarily a fern man, like John and Robbin—his special interest is in the Anacardiaceae, a family of flowering plants with oily resins, and he has studied these all over the world. Poison ivy, *Toxicodendron,* is the best known one. But many others in this family can cause toxic reactions too—the cashew-nut tree, the mango tree, the Brazilian pepper tree, the Japanese wax tree, the Chinese lacquer tree (I had never been sure where lacquer came from, and in Mexico, I heard, it was made from an insect). Many of their resins, J.D. tells me, have industrial or medical uses, like the dhobi or marking-nut tree, whose liquid is used as an indelible ink to mark laundry. And cashew-nut shell liquid is used to control mosquito larvae and as an antimicrobial agent. "A wonderful family!" J.D. exclaims, in conclusion.

But now his attention comes back to the plant in front of him. "This is the greatest thrill for me—I never thought I would see *Pseudosmodingium,* actually see it growing." He goes on to speak of a toxin it has. "It's horrible. Never been analyzed. You get a terrible rash, internal troubles too, ulcers. Poison ivy is nothing compared to it. I should have had my rubber gloves with me." He specifically brought thick rubber gloves for such an eventuality, and today—of all days!—he forgot to bring them. "Would you imagine there was such an exciting thing?" he goes on. He will see if he can return here, tomorrow, take a taxi, no matter what it costs—bringing the rubber gloves with him.

The spring percolates through a whole mountain of limestone before it bubbles out from the side of the mountain into a huge basin, and from here it tracks downward, depositing lime and other minerals as it goes, until it makes its final drop from a semicircle of cliffs. But by this time, with evaporation and absorption, the water is so saturated with minerals that it crystallizes, turns to stone, as it falls—thus the "petrified water-fall." It is an amazing simulacrum of a waterfall, consisting not of water but of the mineral calcite, yellowish-white, hanging in vast rippling sheets from the cliffs above. There are pools of the warm, mineral-rich water at the summit. I long to immerse myself, at least paddle, in this concentrated water. But I fear to intrude my dirty, alien germs in this innocent, pristine habitat. John Mickel bestows a brief glance at this unique natural spectacle, the only such (someone says) in the entire world, and then attends to the varied ferns at the top. He finds some new (at least new to me, to us) xerophytic ferns on the rock—a very hand-some silvery *Argyrochosma* (I misheard this as "Argyrocosmos," and thought of a silver universe) and an *Astrolepis integerrima,* both des-iccated, but alive, next to each other on the blue-gray rock.

What fascinates me equally are the mosses and the tiny heart-shaped liverworts adhering to these bone-dry rocks. I would not have thought such things possible, for one thinks of these (liverworts above all) as quintessentially moist and moisture-loving plants, among the first plants to make it onto land, but having (one would think) no way of conserving water or otherwise protecting themselves, for they have such thin and delicate tissues. But they are evidently able to survive the dry season, apparently quite as well as the xerophytic ferns. The question is—must ask John—whether flowering plants can do as well as these "primitives" in this sort of suspended animation.

On the way back from the falls, I join J.D. again, who is all excited at seeing a Mexican pistachio, *Pistacia vera,* which, he says, hails from Central Asia. This too belongs to "his" family, the Anacardiaceae. "This is so exciting," he murmurs. "No Anacardiaceae till today—and now two!"

Between identifying these plants (and many others, including a beautiful blue *Wigandia,* a member of the waterleaf family), J.D. continually spots different birds, is preternaturally skilled at seeing and following them—often tiny hummingbirds, hundreds of yards away—whereas I can see nothing smaller than hawks or vultures.

As the bus heads back to Oaxaca I gaze idly out the window— fields of agaves; old women in dark shawls, moving in the fields, checking the agaves; thatched cottages shaped like beehives. Some of the roofs on the larger ones are reinforced with cornstalks—this (I am told) insulates them better. In one field there is a satellite dish rising from the cornstalks—a surreal twenty-first-century thing, cheek by jowl with a natural form of roofing, unchanged for thousands of years. I try to photograph this, but, missing—we are going too fast—attempt a tiny sketch in my notebook.

We arrive back at the hotel in midafternoon, ready to share all of our botanical findings with one another in a sort of show-and-tell.

We sometimes do this at our Saturday AFS meetings back in New York, but here we have so many riches that it will take hours to show them all.

Some of the dried-up, seemingly dead ferns gathered the day before have been left in water overnight: the *Astrolepis*, the

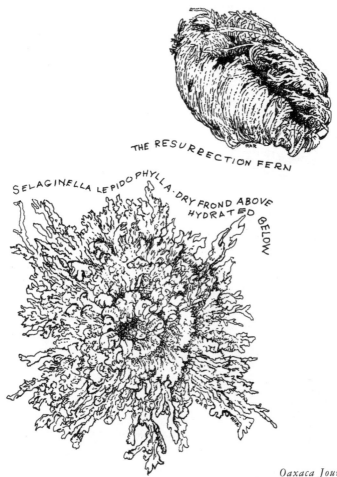

THE RESURRECTION FERN

SELAGINELLA LEPIDOPHYLLA. DRY FROND ABOVE HYDRATED BELOW

Notholaena, a *Cheilanthes,* and, of course, the resurrection fern—all of these, after a good soaking, have miraculously turned green, expanded and uncurled like Chinese water flowers.

Robbin has brought some segments of tree fern trunks all the way from New York, in order to bring out a point. We had all seen such segments in the market and elsewhere; they are widely sold throughout Mexico, as containers for orchids, and professional orchid growers in Mexico and the U.S. use them by the thousand. But this, of course, involves the destruction of the plant itself, and tree ferns in Mexico are now endangered by the practice. The tree fern trunks he has brought are very beautiful in cross-section, because six or seven vascular bundles run up the stem, their black sheaths in dramatic contrast with the white pith and cortex around them.

Pteris podophylla

Many treasures have been brought back from the Atlantic slope expedition, which I missed yesterday. Robbin had looked by my room the previous evening—exhausted, but elated, having been on the road for sixteen hours—with a beautiful, giant frond of *Pteris podophylla,* and a *Psilotum* which he had seen growing on a tree fern, one fern growing on another. Now I see these and many more specimens, carefully laid out on a table.

John Mickel shows us a frond

from a rare *Elaphoglossum*—he risked his life, apparently, crawling far out on a tree limb to get it; the tree limb cracked under his weight, almost precipitating him below. These enthusiasts think nothing of risking their limbs and lives for ferns—and they are astoundingly agile. Here is John, in his mid-sixties, leaping brooks, scrambling up cliffs, climbing trees, like a boy—and this is so for almost all the party, including some who are ten years his senior.

There are several species of *Botrychium*, including one never before described. If only I had been there, been at the discovery! Discovering a new species is the high point of a field botanist's life, almost the equivalent of a chemist discovering a new element. Perhaps the new species of *Botrychium*, if it is a new species, and not merely a variant, will be named for Herb Wagner—a teacher of John's and Robbin's, and a long-standing and

ELAPHOGLOSSUM GLAUCUM

BACK SIDE OF FROND SHOWING SPORANGIA

RAR

much loved member of the AFS, who died earlier this month. Or perhaps after our beloved Eth Williams.

Eth Williams has been very much on my mind, on all our minds, for she too died, at ninety-five, just a few days before we left, and we are, all of us, bereft. The fern society meetings will never be the same now that she is gone. Eth and her husband, Vic, were there at the first meeting of the New York chapter, and she became its president in 1975. She would come to every meeting, bringing along dozens of little ferns that she had raised from spores in her greenhouse—beautiful, and sometimes quite rare, ferns which she sold or auctioned for a nominal dollar or two. She had the greenest thumb of anyone I ever met: She would sow the spores on sterilized peat pellets, keep them in a humidity chamber until they sprouted, and then prick the tiny sporelings into little pots. She could coax spores into growing where no one else succeeded, and she was responsible for providing not only the ferns at our meetings, but all the spore-grown ferns in the New York Botanical Garden's collection for the past twenty-five years, working at first by herself, and then with a devoted group of five volunteers, the "Spore Corps."

A great hiker in her younger days, Eth had started using a stick at the age of ninety, but remained upright and very active, with a dry, charming humor and total clarity of mind to the last. She knew all of us by name, and was for all of us, I suspect, a sort of ideal aunt, or great-aunt, the quiet center of every meeting. She and Vic had married in the 1950s and were both avid field botanists. When a new Peruvian species of *Elaphoglossum* (she was particularly fond of these) was found in 1991, John named it *E. williamsiorum* in honor of them both.

Someone else exhibits some filmy ferns which she found in the Oaxacan rain forest. Eth, I cannot help thinking, would have loved these delicate things: Only one cell thick, these ferns require nearly constant 100 percent humidity, so they cannot grow anywhere except in a rain forest (I have seen them in Pohnpei, and in Guam, too). There are at least ten species of these lovely, diaphanous, infinitely delicate *Hymenophyllum* growing in the Oaxaca rain forest.

A whole banquet of *Polypodium*, the "many-footed" fern, have been collected—*martensii, plebeium, longepinnulatum*—but, John says, there are more than fifty species here if one is really looking, not just the nineteen noted in our list.

Dick Rauh shows us the beautiful fern drawings he has been doing—thirty or more, each a few inches square, on a long zigzag of paper which folds up like a concertina. I am especially enchanted by his drawing of the resurrection fern, and by a drawing of the dramatic scene I missed the previous day, of John Mickel outstretched on a high branch, risking his life to get his *Elaphoglossum*.

Scott and Carol have prepared an exhibit of local fruit and vegetables and other foods. They also have some castor "beans," which look like bloated ticks, the seeds of the euphorb *Ricinus communis*. Though the castor bean hails from Africa, they tell us, it is now cultivated in large amounts in Mexico, too, for the oil has innumerable uses: as a lubricant in engines (including the racing oil, Castrol), as a quick-drying oil used in paints and varnishes, as a water-resistant coating for fabrics, a raw material in the production of nylon, a lamp oil, and not least, as a gentle purgative (I am reminded of childhood, and the doses of castor oil I was sometimes forced to swallow). But while the oil is benign, the seed itself is lethal, because it contains ricin, thousands of times more toxic than cobra venom or hydrogen cyanide. This stirs memories, and we all reminisce about the mysterious death in 1978 of Georgi Markov, a dissident Bulgarian journalist, in a London street. Markov died an agonizing death three days after being jabbed in the leg at a bus stop with the sharp ferrule of an umbrella. Scotland Yard later established that the umbrella jab, far from being accidental, had delivered a pellet the size of a pinhead containing ricin.

While Scott is primarily a plant systematist and Carol is primarily a plant photographer, both are very knowledgeable about the economic uses and natural history of plants. It is lovely to see their complementary enthusiasms and interests. I have a special feeling for these botanical couples who are both spouses and working partners; they seem much more romantic to me than medical couples, like my parents. I find myself wondering how these couples met, and at what point their shared botanical enthusiasm became enthusiasm for each other. I am especially touched by Barbara Joe and Takashi Hoshizaki, who are now, I guess, both in their seventies, having spent a half-century or more of inseparably mixed botanical and married life together. Takashi is Japanese-American, born in California, and he tells frightening stories of how he and his family, most of his neighbors, were forced to live in internment camps during World War II. Barbara Joe, also a California native, is a Chinese-American, and such mixed marriages, in their generation, were rare. They met as students in Los Angeles, and when they married, Takashi designed a house for Barbara Joe which would accommodate her ferns—from any spot inside the house, she can look out onto lush, ferny plantscapes, and there is a greenhouse for the delicate ones. While both of them are primarily interested in ferns, Barbara Joe is above all drawn to the description and classification of ferns, their filiation and taxonomic relationships. She is the national president of the American Fern Society, and the author of a beautiful and encyclopedic book called *Fern Grower's Manual* (she is currently working on a new edition of this with Robbin). Takashi is more drawn to plant physiology, but he has other, unexpected interests as well. He worked for many years at the Jet Propulsion Laboratories in Pasadena, and is an expert in the mechanisms of flight. A genius with models and simulations, he once made an artificial condor which was so realistic that when he set it on long flights around Los Angeles, there were puzzled reports about giant condors in the area. The Hoshizakis have pressed me to visit them in Los Angeles, where, they promise, I will be shown the magic fern garden they have created around their house.

I have also observed—I was a little slow to see it—two lesbian couples, and one gay couple, in our group. Very stable, long-term, as-if-married relationships, solidified, stabilized, by a shared love of botany. There is an easy, unselfconscious mixing here of all the couples—straight, lesbian, gay—all the potential intolerances and rejections and suspicions and alienations transcended completely in the shared botanical enthusiasm, the togetherness of the group.

I myself may be the only single person here, but I have been single, a singleton, all my life. Yet here this does not matter in the least, either. I have a strong feeling of being one of the group, of belonging, of communal affection—a feeling that is extremely rare in my life, and may be in part a cause of a strange "symptom" I have had, an odd feeling in the last day or so, which I was hard put to diagnose, and first ascribed to the altitude. It was, I suddenly realized, a feeling of joy, a feeling so unusual I was slow to recognize it. There are many causes for this joyousness, I suspect—the plants, the ruins, the people of Oaxaca—but the sense of this sweet community, belonging, is surely a part of it.

CHAPTER SEVEN

THURSDAY

Today I pay more attention to the vegetation of the valley as we drive through it—the serried, upright organ-pipe cactus and the prickly-pear, nopal cactus. These cacti form an integral part of the culture—the nopal pads are sliced and cooked (I have had them as a vegetable with almost every meal), and their strawberry-like fruits make very sweet, tasty jelly or jam. The ancient pictographs are full of cacti. An eagle perched on a nopal eating a snake, for example, which the Aztec saw as the sign from the gods that they had arrived, found a place to settle, in 1325. We saw such an image a few days ago, as a giant painting on the face of a cliff near Yagul. In pre-Hispanic days, Luis tells us, seems almost to recollect—at times he seems to contain the entire history of his people in himself—snakes were sacred symbols, earth symbols; they changed their skins as the Earth changed seasons. But in Christian tradition, the serpent became evil, the tempter. Snakes, once revered, were deliberately killed after the Spaniards came.

Then there are the spiky agaves and yuccas. There are acacias, lots of them. John Mickel warns us to treat them with respect, for some of them host colonies of symbiotic ants, and these will furiously attack anyone who messes with their home. There is a fine tall grass, *Arundo donax,* with spear-shaped blades, some of which are eight feet high or more. This may be used for thatching, or roofs, perhaps for carpets, mats, too. Then there is the dangerous bad woman (*Mala mujer*)— *Cnidoscolus,* a nightmare plant of the euphorbia family covered with poisonous hairs. I had heard this spoken of, its use by pranksters, by my neighbor in the plane, but John warns us solemnly against even the slightest accidental touch.

Lime trees, pomegranates, hedges of organ-pipe. Most families have small holdings with a few goats, burros, corn, agave, prickly pears. Most? Or just a few. A burro, Luis says, may be (relatively) more costly than a car is in the States. Poverty is everywhere evident here.

The garbage in the streets, the negligent filth in the hills, Luis says, are moral residues of colonialism, reflecting the people's sense that the streets, the cities, the lands, are no longer theirs. He goes on to speak of the state as huge, inefficient, corrupt. How the police are paid so little that it is natural they should accept fifty or a hundred pesos for overlooking an infraction at a red light, for this is as much, or more than, their daily pay. He speaks of drug mafias as being in cahoots with the police. The police, he says, are as much feared as the criminals.

Higher, higher, now—a mountain valley filled with palms, fields of agave.

Near Mitla, Luis tells us as we drive through the valley, there are a few small villages with relatively pure-blooded Indians. There are only three groups of truly pure-blooded Indians left: one in the rain forests of Chiapas, one in Oaxaca in the cloud forest, and one in the north of Mexico. There are no roads to these villages, and they are remote, a one- or two-day trek through the mountains. Their ancestors fled at the time of the Conquest, and they had survived only through isolation; for them, at least, there was dignity, autonomy, whereas if they had stayed in Oaxaca, they would have been slaves.

Within fifty years of the conquistadors' arrival, Luis continued, the native population was decimated. Disease, murder, demoralization—entire peoples committed suicide in order to avoid enslavement, regarded death as preferable. Most of those remaining intermarried with the Spaniards, so that almost all Mexicans today are mestizos. But the mestizos were not recognized legally by the colonial governors—they had no rights, and their property could not be inherited by their children, but instead reverted to the state.

Life under Spanish rule was becoming intolerable, and revolt, revolution, was becoming inevitable. In 1810 it started, on September 16, the date still celebrated as Mexico's independence day. The revolution was started, Luis said, by a parish priest, who rang the church bell to rally his villagers, shouting "Long live our Lady of Guadalupe! Death to bad government! Death to the Spaniards!" But it was eleven years before independence was finally achieved in 1821, only to usher in several decades of chaos, under a succession of ineffective rulers, during which time Mexico lost half its territory—Texas, California, Arizona, and New Mexico—to the United States.

Then a brief halcyon period, just five years, between 1867 and 1872, under the benign rule of Benito Juárez. Like his contemporary, Abraham Lincoln, Juárez had a moral grandeur—his guiding principle was "Respect for the rights of others means peace"—and he fought for democracy as well as independence from European rule.

A few years after the death of Juárez came the accession of Porfirio Díaz, a despot who ruled Mexico for thirty-five years. Díaz, Luis explained, was a deeply ambiguous figure: a general, a dictator, ruthless, paranoid, who nonetheless organized roads and industries, bridges, buildings. The country grew more productive, moved into step with the rest of the modernized world, but at a terrible human cost: There was virtual enslavement in factories and on haciendas, huge corruption and profiteering.

Entering the village of Mitla, we see a dog running through the streets, with one leg tied to a goat. We find ourselves surrounded by dogs, as everywhere in Mexico. One of them has a broken leg—I wonder how this happened, how it will survive. Children hold out their hands and call "¡Peso, peso!" as we pass. Suddenly, we have to brake heavily. There is a religious procession just ahead, making its slow way to the church. I get off the bus, several of us do, and join the procession. People are holding votive candles, flowers, palm fronds. They move slowly, dogs, babies, and cripples among them, to the church, which peals its welcome loudly as they enter. Rockets are set off, dogs bark suddenly, startled; I, too, wince.

Luis, though himself a pious Catholic, murmurs darkly about these processions. "Bread and circuses," he says, "to distract the masses." The church here, he feels, is without courage or power. It offers bread and circuses—processions—to pacify the people, but otherwise passively supports a corrupt government. "I say this," concludes Luis, "even though I am a Catholic—I believe in my religion, but I am heartbroken and angry about our Church here."

It is not the ruins of Mitla that immediately capture our attention, but the piled trunks of organ-pipe cacti outside the site. Such trunks are often uprooted to make fencing, and once "planted," they may reroot and proliferate. (I am reminded of how, in New Zealand, the stems of tree ferns are used as fencing in this way, and how these too shoot out fronds, becoming a rich living hedge.) An impromptu conference on the subject of living fences—the archaeological wonders of Mitla will have to wait.

Building with plants having received an exhaustive discussion, we now raise our eyes to the church before us—a church built by the Spanish upon the older site and using stones from the buildings they destroyed. Mitla was still active, Luis is saying, when the Spaniards came. The conquistadors tended to raze entire cities, symbolically building their own churches on top of the original foundations. Mitla was partly spared, but a new Mitla had been built on top of the old one, using, cannibalizing, the original stones. Succeeding generations have continued to cannibalize, to exploit, their own past.

But where Yagul—at least all that is now left of it—has been largely destroyed, leaving only its ground plan and some low, half-crumbled structures, here at Mitla there are the remains of an entire palace still standing, with gigantic, yard-high steps leading up to it. It has dozens of interconnecting rooms, and must have seemed incredible when archaeologists first discovered its labyrinthine entirety.

The walls of the palace are composed of adobe—sticky clay mixed with stalks of corn, animal stools, all fermented together —and conical stones pressed into it, so as to form an elastic base—the stones can move independently in their matrix of adobe, absorbing, dispersing, the force of an earthquake. I am fascinated by this, and draw a diagram in my notebook: the discovery of composites for added strength, for resisting shock, millennia ago. Since nothing so singular can be passed over by the group, a vigorous discussion at once breaks out about composites in nature—the interweaving, at a microscopic level, of two different materials, one crystalline or amorphous, perhaps, and one fibrous, in order to get something harder, tougher, yet more elastic than either component alone. Nature has employed composites in all sorts of biological structures: horses' hooves, abalone shells, bone, the cell walls of plants. We use the same principle for reinforced concrete, and new synthetic ceramics or reinforced plastics; the Zapotec used it for adobe.

The huge stone crosspiece above the palace door weighs at least fifteen tons—it was cut locally, but how was it brought here? There were no domestic animals, there was no use of the wheel (except, curiously, for toys)—presumably they used rollers, as the Egyptians did for the pyramids. But how did the

Zapotec cut and shape these stones with such fineness? They had no iron, no bronze, no smelting—only native metals, silver, gold, copper, all too soft to cut stone. But the great Mesoamerican equivalent for metal was volcanic glass, obsidian. It was with obsidian blades, presumably, that they did all their surgery, and the Aztec their grisly human sacrifices, too. I buy a cruel-looking, sharp-edged shard of obsidian as we go out—black, translucent at its thinnest, with the conchoidal fracture characteristic of all glasses.

The doorways between the palace rooms are low (and made lower by the steel braces which have been inserted to support them). But the ceilings, the tops of the walls, have exquisite, complex, geometrical figures—I copy some of these into my note-book—tessellations, ramparts, like the visual "fortification" patterns one may get during a migraine, and complex hexagonal and pentagonal patterns. I am reminded of patterns in Navajo rugs, or Moorish arabesques. Normally one of the more silent members of the group—who am I to speak up in so erudite a group?—I am stimulated by the geometric figures around us to speak of neurological form-constants, the geometrical hallucinations of honeycombs, spiderwebs, latticeworks, spirals, or funnels which can appear in starvation, sensory deprivation or intoxications, as well as migraine. Were psilocybin mushrooms used to induce such hallucinations? Or the morning glory seeds common in Oaxaca? People are startled by my sudden loquacity, but intrigued by the notion of universal hallucinatory form-constants, a possible neurological foundation for the geometrical art of so many cultures.

But there is, as always, a limit—and after twenty minutes of traversing the rooms, admiring the achievements of pre-Columbian art and architecture, the group is eager to go outside, to look at what really matters—the vegetation. Indeed the professionals—Scott, with his camera and notebook, David Emory in his brightly colored suspenders, with his "third" eye, his hand lens—have avoided entering the palace in the first place, and devoted themselves to botanizing outside it. Scott again points out wild nicotine, a non-indigenous grass (*Tricholaena rosea*) introduced from Africa, some goosefoot, a prickly poppy with a delicate yellow color—and a parasitic wasp of enormous size. Robbin points out a little yellow star-shaped flower, one of the Zygophyllaceae—its four-pointed fruit resembles a caltrops. One point is always sticking up, he shows me, and will pierce the footpad of a passing animal (like the medieval weapon), and so be transported elsewhere. I am delighted to hear the word "caltrops" still in use—it is a word I am rather fond of, partly because it is a singular noun ending in "s," like *Cacops* and *Eryops,* my favorite fossil amphibians.

We return to the bus. It has become very hot now, in the middle of the day, and as we bus back I see two boys with bikes, talking together under the shade of a tree. I reach for my camera, but it is too late. It would have made a charming picture.

We have now driven from Mitla to Matatlán, a village full of backyard mescal makers. The agave—*maguey*—is to Central Americans what the palm is to Polynesians. Its very name (our name), agave, means "admirable." Carlos V's envoy extolled it in 1519: "Surely nature has never combined in one plant so central, so revered, so enthralled by everybody," and Humboldt described it in equally lyrical terms three centuries later. For the maguey not only provides fiber for ropes and coarse fabrics, and thorns for sewing, but sweet, odorous pulp for fermentation. Distillation was unknown before the Spaniards, and thus there was only *pulque,* a freshly fermented brew from the maguey (and one which could not be kept, but had to be drunk immediately after fermentation). As we drive from Mitla, we pass fields of maguey, some on waterless slopes which would not support any other crop.

Some of the magueys have tall flower stalks with greenish or cream-colored flowers. A few have bulbils instead of flowers, and these can grow directly into new plants. John tells us how the vegetative buds are planted in a nursery for two years, then transferred to the field for another eight years. At harvest, all the leaves are removed and the stem is cut at ground level. The stems—*piñas*—often contain maguey worms, and these are removed and put in the mescal as a special delicacy.

Of the many new foods I have eaten in the past days, the grasshoppers have pleased me especially—crunchy, nutty, tasty, and nutritious; they are usually fried and spiced.* After getting

---

* Grasshoppers, by a special biblical dispensation, are kosher, unlike most invertebrates. (Did not John the Baptist live on locusts and wild honey?) This always seemed to me a reasonable, even necessary, dispensation, for life in ancient Israel was quite chancy, and locusts, like manna, were a godsend in lean times. And locusts could come in uncountable millions, wiping out the always precarious harvests of the time. So it seemed only just, a poetic and nutritional justice, that some of these voracious eaters be eaten themselves.

Yet I was outraged, as well as amused, when I visited the Pantanal in Brazil a couple of years ago, to find that the capybaras there, giant aquatic guinea pigs—sweet, herbivorous animals minding their own business—were at one point almost wiped out because of a special papal dispensation which decreed that, for purposes of Lent, these mammals could be regarded as "fish," and thus eaten. Not only a monstrous sophistry, but one that drove the gentle capybara almost to extinction. (Beavers in North America, Robbin tells me, were also classified as "fish" for the same reason.)

used to these, I am ready to try a maguey worm—we see baskets of these, writhing, when we go to the distillery. They look something like the live Klingon worms eaten on *Star Trek.*

Why stop at grasshoppers and worms, I wonder? A quarter of the earth's animal mass consists of ants. This is a menace (since they produce a great deal of methane, which enlarges the ozone hole), but it is also, potentially, a huge source of food. If they could be divested of their formic acid or whatever, they could feed the starving masses. Ant larvae, I am told, are in fact a delicacy in expensive Mexico City restaurants.

(One insect, however, is *not* to be eaten. One must not swallow a firefly. Swallow three fireflies, it is said, and you're a goner. They contain a substance with digitalis-like actions, but intensely potent, not to be trifled with.)

There are at least a score of mescal distillers in Matatlán alone, most small backyard operators. A heavy smell of fermenting maguey perfumes the entire village—one could get high by merely breathing the air. We visit one distiller whose gaily colored awning fronts the main road. Here we see the piñas, the maguey stems, covered with gunnysacks and earth in a pit in his front yard; a fire is built here, and the piñas are cooked for three days. This converts their starch to sugar—they are delicious to eat now, and are eaten, especially by children, like sugarcane. The cooked stems are ground on a round stone platform with a millstone—a mule is used to pull it. Then the mash is put into large vats to ferment. It bubbles, heavy bubbles of carbon dioxide, and starts to become alcoholic—the bubbly mass is then cooked in a large copper kettle for three hours, and the distillate collected below. The particular distiller we are visiting makes "straight mescal" (which is 98 proof, almost 50 percent alcohol), and *pechuga,* mescal flavored by raw chicken breasts. This is more delicate in taste, and highly esteemed—but the idea of raw chicken breasts disturbs me here, a mixing of categories, as would the notion, for example, of fish-flavored gin. There are also more liqueurlike forms flavored with plum, pineapple, pear, and mango. We are given liberal samples of all these to try—and the effect on our empty stomachs is immediate and strong. A strange joviality overcomes everyone—we smile at each other, we laugh at nothing. We spend two hours tippling (and buying absurd trinkets) in the middle of the day. This is the first time I have seen our somewhat austere and intellectually dedicated group let themselves go, relax, giggle, be silly.

Heated with alcohol, tipsy, famished, we drive on to La Escondida, a famous restaurant where there is an enormous buffet of more than a hundred different dishes to choose from, some of them visually intriguing, surreal, and almost none of them recognizable. I have almost the sense of being on another planet. Should I concentrate on one dish, or half a dozen, or try them all? I decide I want to try them all, but after twenty or so I realize it is beyond me. One would have to come here once a week for a year and sample a different selection each time. I know Oaxaca has the richest flora in Mexico. I see now it has the richest, most varied foods as well. I think I am beginning to fall in love with the place.

Sated, swollen, half-drunk as well, I have a strong desire to lie down and sleep. Outside the restaurant I do see a man asleep at the wheel in his car—a physician, I note, from a plate in the windshield. He is frighteningly motionless and looks to me pale—is he just having a snooze, asleep, or is he in coma, even dead? Should I go over to the car, tap him on the shoulder? Perhaps the tap might show him unwakeable, topple his now inanimate body from the wheel. But perhaps he would be furious at being woken like this. What would I say? Just checking, just wanted to make sure you were not dead—ha, ha, with a nervous, apologetic laugh. Knowing no Spanish I do nothing—but as the bus draws out a few minutes later, I cast a long, last glance at him. He is still lying, motionless, against the wheel in his baking car.

The entire village of Matatlán is dedicated to the distilling of mescal, and this sort of specialization is common; this mosaic of specialized villages, this economic organization, is pre-Columbian in origin. Thus everyone in Arrazola carves wood; everyone in Teotitlán del Valle is a weaver, and everyone in San Bartolo Coyotepec, where we have now arrived, makes the black pottery which Oaxaca is justly famous for. We watch a young man create a jug, without using a potter's wheel—a pre-Columbian technique. He attaches a handle and then, with a gesture at once deft and light, suddenly pulls the lip into a beak. The clay needs three weeks to dry. There is no glazing, but rather a sort of polishing, with what looks like a lump of quartz, then the pottery is fired at 800°F in a closed oven, which restricts the oxygen available. This causes the metallic oxides within the clay to convert to their metallic form, and the pottery will take on a brilliant sheen with this.

The ores in the area are especially rich in iron and uranium—
I will be interested, when I return home, to see if these pots
are magnetic, and to test them for radioactivity with a
Geiger counter.

In Teotitlán del Valle, we visit the house of Don Isaac
Vásquez, a master weaver whose carpets and blankets, and use
of natural dyes, have become famous outside Mexico. He lives
and works with his extended family—such families are the
norm here among the artisans; there is almost a hereditary
artisan class. The children will be trained in weaving and
dyeing from an early age. They will be surrounded by it,
imbibe it, consciously or unconsciously, every minute of their
lives. Their skills, their identities, will be shaped from the
start, and not just by the family situation but by the whole
village, the local tradition, in which they grow up.

Seeing Don Isaac at work, and his old mother, who cards
the wool, and his wife, his brothers and sisters, cousins, nieces
and nephews, the half-dozen children in the backyard; seeing
them all work—totally engrossed, employed, in different
aspects of the business, I have a sense of wistfulness, and of
slight disquiet, too. All of them know who they are, have
their identities, their places, their destinies, in the world;
they are the Vásquezes, the oldest and most distinguished
weavers in Teotitlán del Valle, the living embodiments of an
ancient and noble tradition. Their lives are predestined,
almost programmed, from birth—lives useful and creative, an
integral part of the culture about them. They belong.

Virtually everyone in Teotitlán del Valle has a deep and detailed knowledge of weaving and dyeing, and all that goes with it—carding, combing the wool, spinning the yarn, raising the insects on their favorite cacti, picking the right indigo plants. A total knowledge is located, embodied in the individuals, the families of this village. No "experts" need to be called in, no external knowledge which is not already in the village. Every aspect of the expertise is located right here.

How different this is from our own, more "advanced" culture, where nobody knows how to do or make anything for themselves. A pen, a pencil—how are these made? Could we make one for ourselves, if we had to? I fear for the survival of this village, and the many like it, which have survived for a thousand years or more. Will they disappear in our super-specialized, mass-market world?

There is something so sweet and stable about this village of artisans, and its set, fixed place in the culture around it—such villages remain little changed with the passage of time: the sons succeeding their fathers, and in turn succeeded, centuries passing without either development or disruption. A nostalgia for this timelessness, this medieval life, grips me.

And yet, I wonder, suppose one of the young Vásquezes were to have great mathematical ability? Or an impulse to write? Or paint, or compose music? Or just a desire to get out, to see the world, do something different—what then? What conflicts would occur, what pressures brought to bear?

We watch the carding, the combing, the looming of the wool, the weavers at work amid their great wooden looms, but our interests, mine at least, are more in the dyes. Only natural dyes are used, dyes used for millennia before the conquest —most of them are vegetable, and each day a different dye is used. But today is a red day, a day for cochineal.

When the Spaniards first saw cochineal they were amazed —there existed no dye in the Old World of such a rich redness and fullness, and so colorfast, so stable, so impervious to change. Cochineal, along with gold and silver, became one of the great prizes of New Spain, and weight for weight, indeed, was more precious than gold. It takes seventy thousand of the insects, Don Isaac tells us, to produce a pound of dry material. The cochineal insects (only the females are used) are to be found only on certain cacti native to Mexico and Central America—this was why cochineal was unknown to the Old World. Outside Don Isaac's place are prickly pears sedulously sown with the insect which form little hard white waxy cocoons—somewhat like scale—that one can split with a knife (sometimes a fingernail). The insects, extracted, have to be de-waxed, and then crushed—and several of Don Isaac's children are doing this with rollers, crushing the dry powder so it becomes finer and finer—assuming a deep magenta or carmine tint as it does so.

Some 10 percent of this powder, I am told, is carminic acid; I am curious to know the structural formula of this, and how readily it can be synthesized. (After the trip I looked this up and realized that carminic acid would in fact be quite easy to synthesize. But synthesizing it would throw thousands of Mexicans out of work, undermine a traditional industry and artisanship which has been part of Mexico's history for thousands of years.)

This deep magenta or carmine was still not the brilliant color which had captivated the Spaniards, the brave scarlet color that would strike terror into their foes, and that later was used to dye the coats of the Redcoats. Such a bright red only appears when the cochineal is acidified—done here by pouring quarts of lemon juice into it. The sudden change of color is very startling. I dab some of the now-brilliant cochineal on my finger, and am tempted to lick it. This would be fine, Don Isaac says; it is sometimes used in red drinks and lipstick, as well as in the finest red ink. Scarlet ink—ink of cochineal! And, it comes to me, a memory of fifty years ago, that we used cochineal as a stain in our biology days—it had been partly replaced by synthetic scarlet stains, but there was still, in the 1940s, no synthetic quite as brilliant.*

The ground-up powder—almost a pound of it (I hardly dare think of its cost, the sheer human cost of raising seventy thousand insects, picking them off the cacti by hand, rendering them down, drying them, grinding and grinding them)— is tipped into a huge urn of steaming water, heated over a wood fire in the yard, and stirred and stirred till the water becomes blood red, and then the raw wool, in great hanks, is

---

* James Lovelock, in his autobiography, *Homage to Gaia*, tells of his excitement, as a young apprentice in a dye-works, preparing carmine from cochineal beetles. The quantities involved were heroic—a 112-pound sack of the beetles had to be ladled into a huge copper vat filled with boiling acetic acid ("it looked like the pictures I had seen of equipment in an alchemist's laboratory"), and after four hours of simmering, the dark red-brown liquor had to be decanted and treated with alum, then ammonia. Adding the ammonia precipitated the carmine lake, which he had to filter, wash, and dry. Now, at last, he had the pure carmine powder, and this, he writes, had "a pure red colour so intense that it seemed to draw the sense of colour through my eyes from my brain. What a joy to participate in the transmutation of dried beetles into immaculate carmine! I felt…like the sorcerer's apprentice."

lowered into it. It will take two or three hours to absorb the dye fully. Looking at the gorgeous reds around me I grow wistful, covetous—Would it be possible, I ask, for my T-shirt to be dyed red? I give them my gray cotton NYBG T-shirt, and within minutes it has become a delicate pink. I wonder how deep the color will become, but I am told that cotton, as opposed to wool, does not absorb the dye too well. But soon I will have, I think with excitement, the only cochineal T-shirt in the world!

I make a blood red smear of cochineal in my notebook, like the smears of chemicals I used to (consciously or accidentally) get on my chemistry books in my school days.

CHAPTER EIGHT

FRIDAY

L ast night there was a magical ending to the day, in the
form of a spectacular total lunar eclipse. A group of us
walked up the steep path by the hotel, to the observatory
which tops the hills (no longer ideal, I would think, with the glow
of city lights). We disposed ourselves on the rocks and ground,
some of us with binoculars and spyglasses (I had my monocular),
and bottles of mescal, and turned our gaze to the full moon above
us. The night was cloudless, the viewing perfect. Robbin poured
out mescal all round, and, looking up, warmed by the liquor, we
howled and bayed at the full moon, wondering how wolves, other
animals, might feel as the moon, their moon, was stolen from
them. We wondered too how such eclipses were understood or
regarded by the Zapotec and the Aztec—and whether the power
of their priests, the awe in which they were held, might have
derived in part from their ability to predict such events.

Later I left the group and found another place to watch when about half of the moon was gone, because I wanted to see "finality" by myself—that strange moment (actually five minutes or so) when there is only the narrowest crescent of light, and this seems to transilluminate the rest of the moon, so that it looks like a dimly lit glass ball, a huge luminous sphere of glass in the sky, with crack lines one never normally sees, and all suffused with that strange reddish penumbra which one always sees with such intensity at finality in an eclipse.

··········

Today we go to the grand ruins at Monte Albán, and in preparation I have been reading a bit about it in my guidebook, about how it was founded in Olmec times, around 600 B.C.— more or less at the same time as Rome; how it had rapidly become a center of Zapotec culture, the political and commercial center of the region, its power extending for two hundred kilometers in every direction from the vantage point of its unique mountain plateau. The leveling of a mountaintop to create this plateau was in itself an astonishing feat of engineering, to say nothing of providing irrigation, food, and sanitation for a population estimated at more than forty thousand. This city housed slaves and artisans, vendors and traders, warriors and athletes, master builders and astronomer-priests, and it was the center of a network of trade relations spreading throughout Mesoamerica, a great market for obsidian, jade, quetzal feathers, jaguar skins, and seashells from the Atlantic and Pacific coasts. Mysteriously, still seemingly at the apex of its influence and power, it was rather suddenly abandoned around A.D. 800, after fifteen hundred years of life. Monte Albán, though much older than Mitla or Yagul, was regarded by the Zapotec as sacred, and they managed to conceal it, apparently, from the conquistadors, so that much of it remains, even now, almost as it was the day it was built.

On the outskirts of Monte Albán we see little mounds of pyramidal shape, tombs and little terraces, dotting the hills. These old hills are suffused with human history, a history long preceding that of Oaxaca city itself, which is only seven centuries old. My first impression of Monte Albán is quite overwhelming, and unexpected. The city itself is spacious and immense, an immensity perhaps exaggerated by its uncanny emptiness. From the high plateau one has an aerial view of Oaxaca, a patchwork spread out in the valley below. Here are ruins on a scale as monumental as those of Rome or Athens— temples, marketplaces, patios, palaces—but high up on a mountaintop, against the brilliant blue of a Mesoamerican sky, and utterly different in character. The city is still suffused with a sense of the divine, for it was once a city of God, like Jerusalem— but now it is desolate, deserted. The gods have flown, along with the people, but one can feel that they were once here.

Luis himself is in a sort of trance, which lends a hypnotic quality to his voice as he speaks about Monte Albán, and how the immense platforms and patios of the city echo the contours of the hills and valleys round it, the whole city a model of its natural surroundings. Not just internally harmonious, but in harmony with the land, the land forms, all around.

There is one building that startles me, because it is set at a violent angle to everything else, revolts against the symmetry of the rest. It has a strange pentagonal shape that makes me think of a ship, a spaceship, an enormous one which has crashed here on the airstrip-like top of Monte Albán—or, perhaps, is about to launch itself to the stars. Its official name is Building J, but it is more informally called the Observatory, for its odd angle seems to have been designed to allow the best possible observation of the transits of Venus and its occasional alignments with other planets.

The astronomer-priests of Monte Albán, Luis was saying, devised an intricate double calendar which was soon to become universal throughout Mesoamerica. There was a secular, terrestrial calendar of 365 days (the Aztec later calculated the solar year to be 365.2420 days) and a sacred calendar of 260 days, every day of which had a unique symbolic significance. The two calendars would coincide once every 18,980 days, roughly fifty-two solar years, marking the end of an era—and this was a time of great terror and despondency, marked by a fear that the sun might never rise again. The final night of this cycle was filled with attempts to avert the dread event by solemn religious ceremonies, penances, and (later, with the Aztec) human sacrifices, and a desperate scouring of the heavens to see which ways the stars, the gods, would go.

Anthony F. Aveni, an expert on Mesoamerican astronomy and archaeoastronomy, writes that the Aztec

> ...saw in the heavens the sustainers of life—the gods they sought to repay, with the blood of sacrifice, for bringing favorable rains, for keeping the earth from quaking, for spurring them on in battle. Among the gods was Black Tezcatlipoca, who ruled

the night from his abode in the north, with its wheel (the Big Dipper). He presided over the cosmic ball court (Gemini) where the gods played a game to set the fate of humankind. He lit the fire sticks (Orion's belt) that brought warmth to the hearth. And at the end of every fifty-two-year calendrical cycle, Black Tezcatlipoca timed the rattlesnake's tail (the Pleiades) so that it passed overhead at midnight—a guarantee that the world would not come to an end but that humanity would be granted another epoch of life.

··········

The Aztec priests, in their skywatcher's temple at Tenochtitlán, were doing what the Zapotec astronomer-priests had been doing in Monte Albán a thousand years earlier.

The Aztec were more superstitious, more ridden with a sort of cosmic fatalism than the Zapotec. One can easily work out, from observations in a rare surviving Aztec codex, that the Aztec saw a partial solar eclipse on the afternoon of August 8, 1496, and this, perhaps combined with shooting stars and malign or equivocal conjunctions of the planets, would have filled them with apprehension. It was these apocalyptic fears, no less than the political divisions among them, and their inability to match the steel armor and arms of the Spaniards, Luis felt, that led to their almost fatalistic collapse before the apparition of Cortés and his small band of conquistadors.

All these thoughts crowd into my mind as I gaze at the Observatory, and find myself reflecting on the strange interpenetrations of superstition and science, the mixture of incredible sophistication and naive animistic beliefs that the Mesoamericans embraced. And how much of this we still have in ourselves. All of Mesoamerican life must have been suffused and dominated by a sense of the supernatural no less than the natural—from the great gods who ruled in the heavens and the underworld to the local gods of maize, of earthquakes, of war.

Wandering around Monte Albán, I find myself continually reminded of ancient Egypt—seeing the temples, the raised platforms, the grand bases for pyramids, the whole grand architecture of outwardness and open spaces. Luis speaks of a sense of the sacred, no less than an aesthetic, at work here—a religion of natural forces and forms, which gives shape to the city's spaces as well as its structures. This seems to have been a gentle, reverent, open-air religion (though tied by elaborate synchronicities to the planets, the stars, the whole cosmos)— a religion which had no use for the violences, the human sacrifices, the horrors, of the Aztec. So, at least, Luis affirms.

There was veneration of ancestors here in Monte Albán, as in ancient Egypt, with grand tombs, mausoleums, around the edge of the city; it is a city of the dead, a necropolis, no less than a metropolis. There are also humbler tombs: the narrow graves of parents and grandparents buried in their own houses, so that their spirits could remain with their descendants. One such grave has been laid open in the Monte Albán museum and shows, beneath a glass cover, a seventy-five-year-old woman, shrunken, with decalcified teeth, osteoporosis, and osteoarthritic knees from a lifetime of hard work—kneeling and grinding maize, perhaps. It seems an indignity to be exposed in this way—and yet it gives the place a human reality. What, one wonders, was her life, her inner life, really like?

It is easy to close one's eyes and imagine the vast central plaza of Monte Albán packed with people—twenty thousand people would easily fit here—packed, perhaps, for the weekly market day, such a market as Bernal Díaz saw in Tenochtitlán. Thousands of bodies would be jostling in the plaza, traders and vendors from all over hawking their wares.

My memory suddenly jolts, goes back to the market in Oaxaca, not the vendors and traders, but the beggars outside, poverty-stricken, demoralized. Like them, the man selling oranges to tourists at the entrance of Monte Albán could be a direct descendant of the men who built this place—or of the conquistadors, perhaps of both. The enormity of our crime, the tragedy, overwhelms me. One sees why Columbus and Cortés are execrated, by some, as villains.

Can one reconstruct an identity which was so ruthlessly, so systematically, undermined and destroyed? And what would it mean to even try? The old pre-Columbian languages still exist and are widely spoken, perhaps by a fifth of the population. The basic foods are unchanged—it is still maize, squashes, peppers, beans, as it was five thousand years ago. There are many cultural survivals. Christianity, one has the sense, for all its long history, is still in some ways only a thin veneer. The art and architecture of the past is everywhere visible.

Standing in one of the vast central open spaces in Monte Albán, I imagine the groundswell of an enormous crowd, voices calling in a dozen tongues, temples packed with worshippers, their prayers rising to the sky, while the silent astronomers work in their spaceship-shaped building. I imagine the roar of the throng, perhaps the entire population of Monte Albán, as they crowd into the ball court to watch the sacred game.

It is this, the ball court, and the centrality of the ball game, which seems unique to Mesoamerica, for there were no ball courts in the Old World, either in their cities or their skies. No ball games, and no balls—how can one have a ball game without a decent ball? But this was not a connection I made at first.

The ball court is very beautiful, restored now to its pristine state, an immense oblong of grass with huge "steps" of granite rising high, pyramidally, to either side. Very little is known about the rules or significance of the games which were played here. The Zapotec version of the ball game, Luis says (as opposed to the later, "degenerate" version of the Aztec—but perhaps Luis, as a Zapotec, is biased) was not about rivalry, but was more akin to a ballet, an endless, never-resolved movement between light and dark, life and death, sun and moon, male and female—the endless fight, the dynamic, of the cosmos. There were no winners, no losers, no goals, in such a game.

The ball game, if sublime in its symbolism, was intensely physical too, with teams of five or six players using every part of the body *except* the feet and hands. Players used their shoulders, their elbows, but especially their hips, which were girded with a basketlike arrangement that helped them project and guide the ball. For the ball itself, larger than a basketball, was made of solid rubber and was bruisingly heavy, ten pounds or more. The Aztec version, at least, unlike Luis's vision of the Zapotec form, was a competitive game, and lethal—for the losing (or, sometimes, the winning) captain would be ritually sacrificed and eaten.

But discussion, in our botanical group, moves to the ball, and how the native peoples of Mesoamerica discovered how to extract the latex from indigenous trees, centuries or even millennia before the Spaniards arrived. The Spanish, indeed, were amazed by their first sight of rubber balls: "When they hit the ground, they bounce back in the air with great speed," one astonished explorer wrote in the sixteenth century. "How can this be?" Some explorers thought the balls must be alive; such elasticity, such bounce, had never been seen in the Old World. They had seen the elasticity of a compressed spring, or a stretched bow, perhaps, but had never dreamt of a substance which was intrinsically elastic.

Many plants have a sticky, milky sap, or latex. Left alone, this will dry to a brittle and fragile solid. It must be treated to coagulate the microscopic globules of rubber it contains, yielding a doughy mass which, as it dries, becomes the elastic solid we know as rubber. There is no single rubber tree, but trees in several different families give a suitable latex, and many of these were discovered by the Mesoamericans. The Maya found that they could cut down the *Castilloa elastica* tree, collect the sticky latex in a trough, and then treat it with the acid juice of morning-glory sap (this was peculiarly convenient, since the *Castilloa* tree was often encircled by morning-glory vines). The rubber they made was used not only for the huge balls used in the game, but for little rubber balls which children played with, and for making religious images and figurines, and rubber-soled sandals, and for binding the heads of axes to their shafts.

Unlike chocolate and tobacco, which were brought to Spain by the early explorers and immediately taken up, rubber was slow to make it to Europe. When it did, it was rubber from the Amazonian tree *Hevea,* and it is this which is extensively cultivated now. The first sheets of rolled rubber were brought to France only in the 1770s, where they aroused great interest. Charles Macintosh, in Scotland, saw how rubber could be used to waterproof fabrics, to make "mackintosh," and Joseph Priestley, the discoverer of oxygen, discovered how it could be used to erase pencil marks, as a "rubber." (Only then did the word rubber come into the language—but I think I prefer the wild-sounding French word, *caoutchouc,* with its echoes of the Quechua original.)

It was only in the nineteenth century that the further discovery was made by Charles Goodyear that if one treated the crude gum with sulphur and heated it, a highly pliable, elastic form of rubber could be made. Goodyear, in this sense, "invented" rubber—except that the same invention had been made by the Maya millennia before. (Only very recently was it found that the morning glory contains sulphur compounds which, as in Goodyear's process, are capable of cross-linking the latex polymers and introducing rigid segments into their chains— chains that entangle and interact with one another, producing the elasticity of rubber.)

Half-listening, half-dreaming, I imagine the ball court as it must have been fifteen hundred years ago, in the heyday of Monte Albán, the jostling players using their hips and buttocks with a graceful yet desperate energy, moving the heavy, almost alive ball this way and that, feeling that they mirrored the ball game in the heavens, and that their own movements, their patterns, the constellations they made, were balancing the actions of the cosmos, the lords of death and life.

I am interrupted in these lofty thoughts by the sight of John Mickel swooping on Tomb 105. "*Astrolepis beitelii!*" he shouts in excitement (an *Astrolepis* not previously in our list). The pteridological passion in him is in full force. And indeed, I see, as the rest of us

ASTROLEPIS BEITELII - REHYDRATED FROND ON RIGHT

are exploring Monte Albán, exclaiming over its wonders, three tiny figures are to be seen, in a field, far below: J.D., David, and Scott, all bent double, or crouching, or lying on their faces, examining the minute flora of the region with their hand lenses. With them the ultimate sacrifice is made— the monumental splendor, the sublimity, the mystery of Monte Albán—sacrificed to the humble but peremptory call of cryptogamic botany.

CHAPTER NINE

Saturday

On our way now to Boone's place, in Ixtlán. Woken from a semi-slumber (slumped in the bus, having visions of pyramids, terraces, the ball court, my cortex replaying Monte Albán) by J.D.'s ejaculation, "Birds!" I open my eyes, and see him alert, tense, scanning the scene with eager, expert eyes.

In the slanting golden early-morning light, I see a cabin just off the road with a burro and a crowded yard—but I cannot grab my camera in time. Just as yesterday, at Monte Albán, I saw a lean, beautifully muscled youth, almost naked, standing on a projecting rock above the great arena. He could have been one of the original inhabitants—a young warrior-priest, perhaps, offering himself to the sun. The beauty of the human figure against the splendor of the backdrop made me reach for the camera. I would have "got" him, got the whole scene, but at that very moment someone asked me a question, and when I had dealt with this, the youth, the moment, had gone.

I think about the botanical richness we have seen here, not just of ferns, but all sorts of other things which we take for granted. The conquistadors had lusted for silver and gold, and robbed their victims blind to get these—but these were not the real gifts they brought back. The real gifts, unknown to the Europeans before the conquest, were tobacco, potatoes, tomatoes, chocolate, gourds, chilies, peppers, maize, to say nothing of rubber, chewing gum, exotic hallucinogens, and cochineal....

"A Kodak moment!" John Mickel announces, as the bus stops for a few minutes—we are on a high mountain ridge now, and smaller peaks stretch like a forested ocean beneath us. But everyone else has seized on minutiae, particulars, bestowing only a perfunctory glance at the breathtaking vista. Dick, right in front of me, has got a tiny flower, a *Lobelia,* he thinks, which he is examining minutely with his lens, exclaiming at its beauty and anatomizing it at the same time. Is it the artist or the scientist in him which is aroused by the *Lobelia?* Both, clearly, and they are utterly fused.

It is similar with Robbin who, in the same brief break from the bus, finds a giant pinecone and is now (using my red and green pens) marking out the way its scales are arranged in orderly spirals about the cone, and arranged in fixed numerical series. "If you don't know about Fibonacci series, how can you truly appreciate a pinecone?" he says. (He had earlier made a similar comment about the logarithmic spirals of fern croziers or fiddleheads.)

"Neat," says Nancy Bristow, examining the cone. Nancy is a mathematician and math teacher by profession, but a botanist and a bird-watcher by avocation. I ask her what she means by "neat."

"Elegant...perfectly organized...symmetrical...complete... the aesthetic and the mathematical combined." She searches for different words, different concepts—now that I have forced her to examine her exclamation "Neat!"

"Is the Goldbach conjecture neat?" I ask. "Is Fermat's last theorem?"

"Well," Nancy says, "its proof is messy in the extreme."

"What about the periodic table?" I ask.

"That," says Nancy, "is particularly neat, as neat as a pinecone, with the sort of neatness that only God, or genius, can construct—divinely economical, the realization of the simplest mathematical laws." Nancy and I both fall silent, surprised at the sudden exploration forced on us by the simple word "neat."

A sudden cry of "Birders!" to alert the birders in the bus to black vultures flying overhead. I mishear this as "Murders!" and am amazed it should be shouted in so exuberant a fashion. Everyone laughs at my mistake, especially when I dramatize it: "Wow! Look at all the corpses! There's a great one there—and gee, look there...."

A little past Ixtlán, approaching Boone's house, we are stopped. A jeep with a machine gun is very visible by the road, to the left. A young man in camouflage pants and a T-shirt marked "Policia Judicial" gets on the bus. Now a real soldier, in khakis, with a netted helmet, boots, puttees. Absurdly young-looking —he looks sixteen—like a boy playing at soldiers. He handles his pen awkwardly. He smiles charmingly, very white teeth in his smooth, dark face—but all this time the machine gun is trained on us. John produces papers, identifies us, shows we're kosher—the charming smile stays, and we are allowed to go on. But it could, quite easily, have worked out differently. These boys, with their machine guns, shoot first and ask questions later (one suspects) if there is any serious challenge or ambiguity, for there is a civil war, a revolt, in the state of Chiapas, quite close by, and the army is jittery, trigger-happy, suspicious. I want to photograph the policeman and soldier, but this, I fear, might be seen as an affront, or a challenge.

The stopping (and often searching) of vehicles, and far-from-gentle questioning and searching of passengers, Luis tells us, is increasingly common in Oaxaca. Indeed, we have seen army roadblocks and search squads everywhere, though this is the first time we ourselves have been stopped by one. They are looking for contraband, especially smuggled arms, but also (Luis says) for people with "religious or political agendas," missionaries, insurrectionaries, who intend to stir up trouble—students, too, with "insufficient documentation." No one is above suspicion in times like these.

John, picking up on this, said that our religion was "Botanica," and showed a NYBG badge (they could have used my now cochineal-pink NYBG T-shirt!).

"Hanging *Polypodia* on the rocks," announces John, who, having dealt very coolly with the military, is now back to his botanical self. "We are going," he adds, "to see the genus *Llavea*." I like the name, with its Welsh-looking double "l." No, not Welsh, John corrects me; *Llavea* was named in 1816 in honor of Pablo de la Llave, who traveled and botanized in Mexico two hundred years ago.

Arriving at the gate to Boone's property, we are disgorged from the bus, and start to trek quite steeply upward. We are quite high again, over 7,000 feet, and with the addition now of a slightly fluey bronchitis (several of us have contracted this), I find myself a little short of breath. Boone comes out to meet us—broad-shouldered, compact, not in the least short of breath (but he lives at this altitude, so it is normal for him)—tough, agile, for all his seventy-five-odd years. He is unsurprised to hear about our encounter with the army. He speaks of the current political situation in Mexico, and then immediately asks, "Have you read Locke?" and goes on to speak of Locke's *Two Treatises of Government*. Agriculture, genetics, politics, philosophy: all are admixed in Boone's spacious mind, and his often sudden transitions from one subject to another are natural associations for a mind of this sort. There will be a period in the middle of the day when some of the group will go trekking in the forest, and others, like myself, can stay in the casita—then, I promise myself, I will have a real talk with Boone, who fascinates me more and more, and whom I want to know better. But this wish is frustrated: Two young soil botanists appear—they have just arrived from Norway, and are making a special pilgrimage to see Boone. Boone greets them, welcomes them, in fluent Norwegian—how many languages, for God's sake, does the man know?—and then disappears, closeted somewhere with them.

The casita itself is both dilapidated and charming—ideal for a dedicated visiting scientist, intolerable, perhaps, for anyone else. But then it is not meant for anyone else. There are tangled plants everywhere, there is a lizard in the sink, and there are six bunklike beds almost on top of each other in the bedroom. There is a fine central table for having a conference, and a large covered area outside for the preparation of specimens. There is a stove and a refrigerator, electricity, hot running water. What else should the visiting botanist desire?

What he truly desires is outside, all around him—for the casita is set in rich and varied forest, with sixty-odd species of ferns within a kilometer of the house and more than two hundred within a radius of fifteen kilometers. The dry central valley and city of Oaxaca lie an hour and a half to the south, and the lush rain forest is only two or three hours to the north. There is, in addition, Boone's small farm, where he still grows corn and much else, and his personal garden with everything from grapefruits to rhododendrons, to say nothing of fish ponds and antique statues.

Carol Gracie has picked a passionflower, *Passiflora,* and now gives us an impromptu talk on how it was used symbolically by the Jesuits. The three stigmas stood for the three nails of the Cross; the five stamens stood for the five wounds of Jesus; the ten tepals for the ten Apostles at the crucifixion; the corona for the crown of thorns placed on Jesus's head; and the tendrils for the whips with which he was beaten as he carried the Cross to Calvary. If the good Fathers had a microscope, I thought, they could have found another dozen structures and symmetries which they could have interpreted as symbols of the crucifixion, embedded by God in the very cells of the plant.

I wander out with Scott, Nancy, and J.D. to a grove of passionflowers, an ideal spot for watching the hummingbirds and butterflies and for botanizing in the dense surround. We have barely settled ourselves before J.D. cries out, "A hummer! In the *Cryptomeria*. He's got a band of iridescent green, like emerald."

J.D. and Nancy keep spotting more and more birds—they must have identified more than twenty species in the course of an hour—and exclaiming in wonder as they do so. I look, and see nothing whatsoever. Or, rather, I see some hawks, and some vultures, nothing else—and the tiny stuff they are exclaiming about I miss completely. It's my eyes, I apologize, poor visual acuity. But my acuity is fine—it is the brain that is defective. The eye must be educated, trained—one develops a bird-watcher's, or geologist's, or pteridologist's eye (as I myself have a "clinical" eye).

Scott, meanwhile, with his eye honed to observe animal-plant interactions, identifies ripped flowers in the *Passiflora;* other flowers, seemingly intact, he bisects with his knife, and finds depleted of nectar. "Illegal entry," he says darkly. Bees, most likely, have preempted the hummingbirds, ignored the ants, and stolen the nectar, often damaging the flowers as they did so.

As I admire the neat way Scott bisects the flowers, I hear J.D.'s voice. "Oh, my God, it's a kestrel. It's magnificent." Nancy, hearing me confuse hawks and vultures, tells me of the aerodynamic differences between them, how vultures, as opposed to hawks, hold their wings at a dihedral angle and then rock...*so*. She brings a different point of view (a mathematician's and engineer's point of view) to birds and their flight, whereas J.D. is primarily a taxonomist and ecologist. Nancy's interest in birds and plants only started a few years ago, and she brings her mathematician's mind with her into the field. I am excited to see this, to see how her abstract-mathematical and naturalist's passions are not in separate compartments of her mind, but can join, interact, fertilize each other, as I see now.

David, the jolly chemist-botanist, bellows, Mispickel!" whenever he sees me.

I answer, "Orpiment!"
"Realgar!" he retorts.

EQUISETUM MYRIOCHAETUM

This, like the smacking of hands, high-fiving, is our jovial, arsenical greeting.

I have seen my first giant horsetails in the wild—*Equisetum myriochaetum*—topping my head. John says it can grow to fifteen feet tall. But how big is the stem, I ask? He makes an O with his thumb and forefinger—one and a half centimeters diameter, maximum. I am deeply disappointed. I had hoped he might say like a slender tree trunk, as thick as a young *Calamites*.

David, overhearing, nods. "You really are an old fossil man." (I had told him, earlier, of my interest, my initiation, in paleobotany.) Robbin recounts the story of how Richard Spruce, the great botanical explorer, coming upon a stand of giant horsetails in Ecuador in the early 1860s, spoke of them as having stems nearly as thick as his wrist, as resembling a forest of young larches. "I could also fancy myself," he wrote, "in some primeval forest of *Calamites*." Could Spruce, we wonder, in fact have come across a population of miraculously surviving *Calamites,* the truly treelike giant horsetails which flourished in the Paleozoic, but extinct for 250 million years?

It would seem very unlikely, and yet...not completely impossible. Perhaps he did find them, perhaps they are still there, a secret enclave, in some lost world of Amazonia. This, says Robbin, is a fantasy he sometimes has ("in my more irrational, romantic moments"), and such a thought is one I sometimes have, too. Stranger things have happened, after all: the discovery in 1938 of the coelacanth, a fish supposedly long extinct. The discovery in the 1950s of an entire class of molluscs thought to have been extinct for nearly 400 million years. The discovery of the dawn redwood, *Metasequoia,* or, most recently, of the Wollemi pine in Australia. Robbin speaks of the isolated high plateaus in Venezuela, with rock walls so sheer one has to helicopter to the top. All of these have endemic species, unique plants of their own, plants seen nowhere else in the world.

We regroup in the casita, spread our specimens out. The giant horsetail (though no *Calamites)* outshines all the others in splendor, to my mind. Boone comes by now—he has been with the Norwegian soil scientists all this while—and takes us out to show us the perennial corn, *Zea diploperennis,* he has grown from seed. It was discovered, a tiny patch of it, about fifteen years ago, in Jalisco, and Boone, among others, realized the agricultural potential it had—both as a plant in its own right, and as one whose corn-smut-resistant genes could be transferred to other varieties of corn. It comes to me, as we stand about him, that there is something different about Boone. With his extraordinary technical ingenuity and originality, his immense range of reading and reference, his passionate, lifelong dedication to restoring the self-respect and autonomy of the impoverished farmers of Oaxaca, he is, intellectually and morally, a being of another order. Boone stands beside the high corn, his strong figure casting a diagonal shadow in the afternoon sun, and bids us goodbye. I have the sense of a rare, a heroic and extraordinary figure—the tall corn, the strong sun, the old man, become one. This is one of those moments, indescribable, when there is a sense of intense reality, an almost preternatural reality—and then we are descending the trail to the gate, reboarding the bus, all in a sort of trance or daze, as if we had had a sudden vision of the sacred, but were now back in the secular, everyday world.

We pile out at one point, a point John has marked and borne in mind from his many previous trips to Oaxaca. Here it is, he says, as we get out: *Llavea cordifolia*—you may never see it again. It is confined to southern Mexico and Guatemala. John had spotted this rare endemic the first time he came to Oaxaca, scanning the banks along the road.

I look at the *Llavea*. Just another damn fern, I think (but this is not a thought I would dare express with this group!).* At the same time I see, out of the corner of my eye, something infinitely stranger and (to me) more interesting— *Pinguicula,* the butterwort, a carnivorous plant. Its leaves are

LLAVEA CORDIFOLIA

---

* When I did say this to Robbin later he was quite indignant. *Llavea* was extraordinary, he said, for it bore its reproductive organs, its fertile pinnae, on the same leaf as its sterile pinnae, and the two had completely different shapes. Wild! And its rarity and restricted range made it doubly fascinating. "Not just any fern has these qualities!" he exclaimed.

oval and mucilaginous—I touch them gingerly—little insects get stuck in the mucilage and are gradually digested.

Llavea is not all that rare. But supposing, I ask Robbin, there are only twenty or thirty plants altogether, all in one spot and nowhere else? Would the location be published and divulged? Robbin and Judith Jones, who sits next to him, agree that, in such circumstances, it would not. I mention an exotic cycad, a species of *Ceratozamia,* of which only twenty or so plants were found in Panama—and how the entire population was removed by a collector, rendering the species extinct in the wild. Judith, who runs a fern nursery in the Pacific Northwest, mentions a botanist, Carl English, who claimed to have discovered a new maidenhair fern, a dwarf *Adiantum,* in the 1950s, but would not say where. He was, in consequence, disbelieved—or told he had a "sport," of no special interest. Thirty years later, after his death, a second isolate was found—so, posthumously, he was vindicated. But why had he concealed its location in the first place? His motivation was not commercial—he made no profit, he distributed the spores freely, all around the world; it was, perhaps, partly professional, the desire to establish scientific priority (though undermined, in this case, because no one believed him), and partly protective, to keep the little patch of plants from being destroyed by collectors. Or perhaps, as Judith thinks, he was simply by nature a secretive man.

This leads us, as the bus wends its way through the high mountains, still high above Oaxaca, to a long discussion of openness and secrecy in science, the questions of priority, of piracy, of patents, and of plagiarism. I say that I am happy for my patients to be seen by other colleagues, I welcome any genuine interest in them or their states, but that I have some colleagues who feel very differently, colleagues who would not let me (or anyone else) see their patients, even briefly, because they are afraid they might be "scooped," and whose correspondence is similarly uninformative and guarded. I mention Lavoisier, who was at pains to make careful notes on all his own discoveries, and to place these, sealed, with the Academy of Sciences, so that there could never be any contesting of his priority; but who, on the other hand, shamelessly, or shamefully, appropriated the discoveries of others.

We shake our heads over the complexity of it all.

Coming back from Boone's, exhilarated, exhausted, Robbin and I decide to spend a last night on the town—a final stroll around the zócalo, a final meal in one of its sidewalk cafes. But first we will go to the cultural museum in town, a vast collection of pre-Hispanic artifacts, housed in an enormous seventeenth-century convent. The richness, the range, of the last few days has bewildered us, and we need to see a summary, a synthesis, everything ordered and catalogued before us.

We stop first in the museum's *biblioteca,* a long, long room, and high, stacked up to the ceiling with incunabula and early calf-bound books. There is a sense here of great learning, of tranquillity, of the immensity of history, and of the fragility of books and paper. It was this fragility that made it possible for the Spanish to destroy the written records of the Maya and the Aztec and preceding civilizations almost completely. Their exquisite, delicate, manuscript books of bark had no chance of surviving the conquistadors' autos-da-fé, and they were destroyed by the thousands—barely half a dozen remain. The writings and glyphs inscribed on the statues and temples and tablets and tombs were somewhat less vulnerable, but many of these are still indecipherable to us, or largely so, despite a century of work. Gazing at the fragile books in this library, I think of the great library of Alexandria, with its hundreds of thousands of unique, uncopied scrolls, whose burning lost forever much of the knowledge of the ancient world.

We had learned, in Monte Albán, about Tomb 7, where a fabulous treasure had been discovered, the Mesoamerican equivalent of Tutankhamen's tomb. The treasure itself, now displayed in the museum, is relatively late, for the original eighth-century contents of the tomb had been removed, and the tomb reused in the fourteenth century to bury a Mixtec noble-man and his servants, along with a hoard of gold and silver and precious stones. There are great funerary urns, such as we had seen all over Monte Albán. And exquisite jewelry and orna-ments made of metal—gold, silver, copper, and alloys of these—and of jade, turquoise, alabaster, quartz, opal, obsidian, *azabache* (whatever this was), and amber. Gold was not valued by the pre-Columbians as such, as stuff, but only for the ways in which it could be used to make objects of beauty. The Spanish found this unintelligible, and in their greed melted down thousands, perhaps millions, of gold artifacts, in order to fill their coffers with the metal. The horror of this comes upon me as I gaze at the few artifacts of gold which had been pre-served, through a rare chance, in Tomb 7. In this sense, at least, the conquistadors had showed themselves to be far baser, far less civilized, than the culture they overthrew.

One display case is devoted to the pre-Hispanic cultures' cosmology, with all their gods of sun, of war, of "atmospheric forces in general," of maize, of earthquakes, of the underworld, of animals and ancestors (an interesting conjunction), of dreams, of love, and of luxury.

In another case we find small mirrors made of pyrite and magnetite. How is it that while these Mesoamerican cultures appreciated magnetite for its luster and beauty, they did not discover the fact that it was magnetic, and that, if floated in water, it might act as a compass? Nor the fact that, if smelted with charcoal, it would yield metallic iron?

How strange that these brilliant and complex cultures, so sophisticated in mathematics and astronomy, in engineering and architecture, so rich in art and culture, so profound in their cosmological understanding and ritual—were still in a pre-wheel, pre-compass, pre-alphabet, pre-iron age. How could they be so "advanced" in some ways, so "primitive" in others? Or were such terms completely inapplicable?

If we compare Mesoamerica to Rome and Athens, I was beginning to realize, or to Babylon and Egypt, or to China and India, we find the disjuncture bewildering. But there is no scale, no linearity, in such matters. How can one evaluate a society, a culture? We can only ask whether there were the relationships and activities, the practices and skills, the beliefs and goals, the ideas and dreams, that make for a fully human life.

This has turned out to be a visit to a very other culture and place, a visit, in a profound sense, to another time. I had imagined, ignorantly, that civilization started in the Middle East. But I have learned that the New World, equally, was a cradle of civilization. The power and grandeur of what I have seen has shocked me, and altered my view of what it means to be human. Monte Albán, above all, has overturned a lifetime of presuppositions, shown me possibilities I never dreamed of. I will read Bernal Díaz and Prescott's 1843 *Conquest of Mexico* again, but with a different perspective, now that I have seen some of it myself. I will brood on the experience, I will read more, and I will surely come again.

CHAPTER TEN

SUNDAY

Today, on this final trip, we are traveling south of Oaxaca toward the city of Sola de Vega. For our last collecting we go to a limestone area, to see lime-loving, calciphilic ferns and other plants. I have a certain feeling of exhaustion, at least of narrative exhaustion, but there is no exhaustion of the others' enthusiasm—it is as if they are seeing all these ferns afresh, for the first time. I too enjoy the ferns—and the others' enthusiasm —but with a sense perhaps of the trip's imminent ending, content myself with the making of a list: *Cheilanthes longipila; Cheiloplecton rigidum; Astrolepis beitelii; Argyrochosma formosa; Notholaena galeottii; Adiantum braunii; Anemia adiantifolia;* two species of *Selaginella;* as well as lichens, mosses, tiny agaves, mimosas, and innumerable DYCs.

After ferning we backtrack to El Vado—the ford—to have a final brunch under the bald cypresses by the river.

Magnificent trees, not as large as El Tule, but still wonderful to see them clustered along this thin watercourse (a watercourse which expands and flows over the road in the rainy season, but is still substantial, even in the middle of the dry season now). Little girls, no more than five, are doing laundry in the river. And we are attended by the village dogs, a dozen or more, strikingly different in size, breed, and color—not like the homogenized dingo-like dogs we have seen in other places. They are attracted (as we are, even my quasivegetarian self) by the delicious smell of beef cooking on a wood fire, and we are happy to feed them as we eat. They are curiously polite, for three or four of them will sit or stand around one, patiently at the ready, but fully accepting of being fed in serial order; 1, 2, 3, 4…1, 2, 3, 4. No dog tries to butt in, or take the other's meat—we are very impressed by this social sense, this sense of equity—or is it just hierarchy and dominance? How is it with wild dogs or hyenas, faced with a kill?

Are these dogs owned—individually or communally—or are they semiferal commensals just living in the village? Dogs, I am told, are rarely owned or treated as pets here—most skulk around and scavenge, and people kick them in an offhand way. They look domesticated, and yet I have a frightened feeling as I am eating, surrounded at one point by as many as seven of them. A frightened feeling of their wolfish potential, wondering how readily they could turn wild, and turn on (rather than to) one of us humans. We probably deserve it. (Perhaps there is always, with me, some of this discomfort, this fear, when I am around large dogs. I love dogs, and have a canine, or rather lupine, middle name myself—Wolf. But my first memory is of being attacked and bitten by a dog—our chow, Peter—when I was just two. I pulled his tail while he was eating, gnawing a bone, and he leapt up and bit my cheek.)

Luis's mother has come along for the trip, and helped by Umberto, the driver, and Fernando, his son, she has set up trestle tables by the river. Luis's brother is a butcher, and has provided the marvelous meat; and his mother, a fine cook, has made two grand traditional dishes—*estofado de pollo,* a Spanish chicken stew in almond sauce, and a *mole amarillo,* with pork, spiced with *yerba santa* and *pitiona.* And to wash everything down—the meats and the tortillas—a huge urn of hot cinnamon-flavored Oaxacan chocolate—a chocolate to which, in the past week, I have become completely addicted. The atmosphere of the brunch is very sweet, very easy. We have been together for nine days now, and all know each other. We have worked hard, climbed gullies, leapt streams, and have seen a quarter of the seven hundred-odd fern species in Oaxaca. Tomorrow we will all have to leave this place and go back to our jobs in Los Angeles or Seattle or Atlanta or New York. But for now, there is nothing to do but sit under the great bald cypresses by the river and enjoy the simple animal pleasure of being alive (perhaps the vegetable pleasure, too; feeling what it might be like to live, unhurried, century after century, and still feel youthful at a thousand years old).

My own self-imposed task, or indulgence, the keeping of a journal, is coming to an end. I am amazed that I have kept at it with such pertinacity—but this is my passion, rendering into words. I have made these last notes sitting under a tree—not one of the bald cypresses, but a prickly-pear tree, and John

Bristow (the third John in our group!—as obsessive with his camera as I with my pen) took my picture quietly when he thought I was not looking.

··········

Setting sun, long rays, gilding little Zapotec villages and sixteenth-century churches—a sweet, mild, gently undulating land. This has been a lovely trip. I have not enjoyed one so much for many years, nor can I analyze, at the moment, quite what is so...so right. The soft contours of the weathered hills, beauty. And now, in the gathering dusk, we pass El Tule once again, its enormous bulk dwarfing the old mission just by it.

The soft shadowed hills remind me, oddly, of such hills on Route 50 near Tracy, California, and a photograph I once took of them, in 1960. I feel young again, or, rather, ageless, timeless.

A hand—dark, shapely, muscular—hangs out the window of a bus as we pass it. It is quite beautiful in itself. I am not curious about its possessor.

··········

Dawn is announced by the coming of the brilliant, still-almost-full orb of the moon to my window. It brings a ghostly, diaphanous light to the room every morning around 4:30 and it is still visible now, high in the sky, as we prepare to jolt through the city to the airport, in broad daylight, three hours later.

There are eighteen of us taking the early plane to Mexico City—from there we will scatter all over the States.

John and Carol, and Robbin, have come down to see us off. There are emotional hugs, hopes to meet again, perhaps on a future visit to Oaxaca. I, of course, will see these three in New York in a couple of weeks, but some of the others may not see them again for a long time.

On the way to the airport, I reflect on my trip to Oaxaca. It had been billed as a fern tour, a sort of amplification of the fern forays we often make on summer Saturdays around New York. And it has been this, a wonderful fern adventure, with novelties and surprises, great beauty at every point. It has been a revelation, too, of how deep and passionate the love of ferns can be— I think of John risking his life to get an *Elaphoglossum*—and of how the sharing of such an enthusiasm has bonded us together. We met as virtual strangers, just ten days ago, and we have become friends, a sort of community, in this short time. We break up now, with reluctance and sadness, like a theater troupe when the play is over.

David and I exchange a last M-O-R.

"Mispickel!"

"Orpiment!"

"Realgar!" A grand man. I will write to him, and hope to see him again, sometime.